The
Prairie Schooner
Story

A Little Magazine's First 25 Years

PAUL R. STEWART

UNIVERSITY OF NEBRASKA PRESS

Publishers on the Plains

UNP

FOR
MOLLY

PREFACE

This book has no thesis. It was undertaken in the belief that the little magazine is a powerful force in the encouragement and promotion of American literature, and that it is therefore worthy of close attention. The appearance of *The Little Magazine: A History and a Bibliography,* by Frederick J. Hoffman, Charles Allen, and Carolyn Ulrich (Princeton, 1946), did much to further our understanding of the little magazine. But because of its breadth, that work is necessarily quite general in its treatment of individual magazines. It is hoped that the present study, by focusing on a single magazine and giving intimate detail concerning its purposes and functions, its methods of operation, its difficulties and its achievements, may serve to supplement Hoffman's work. Prior to the present study, no book-length analysis of this sort had been undertaken.

I was first attracted to the *Prairie Schooner* as the subject for such a study because of a long-standing interest in that magazine and its editor. Upon examining the *Schooner,* I found much to commend it for study. In the motives which led to its founding and in the financial difficulties it has experienced, it appears typical of most American little magazines. But its nearly unique longevity gives it a substance not common to little magazines. As a result of its long life and the breadth of its editorial policy, the *Schooner* has encountered more currents in American literature and a wider variety of social, political, and economic conditions than have magazines of shorter duration or more specific direction. It has also, of course, published a larger number and a greater variety of writers.

I do not intend to imply, by selecting the *Prairie Schooner* as the subject for this study, that it is the best of the many little magazines, or the most important. I am primarily concerned with the problems of how one representative little magazine has defined is purposes, how it has overcome obstacles in an attempt to achieve them, and how, to the degree that it has been successful, it has worked for the good of American literature. The answers obtained should shed some light on the little magazine as a whole. If similar studies could be made of other little magazines, we would perhaps reach a fuller understanding of the little magazine's nature and significance.

Because the ultimate aims of this study are broader than a mere description of the *Prairie Schooner,* and because the *Schooner* does function in a tradition, two chapters focus largely on other magazines which are historically or practically related to the *Schooner.* For the sake of perspective, I have attempted in Chapter 1 to give some view of the historical background. The chapter is not intended to be definitive or comprehensive; a careful reader will notice several omissions of earlier magazines as important as those which have been included. I have attempted merely to sketch the lines which seem to lead, culturally and geographically, to a midwestern magazine like the *Schooner.* It would be interesting to draw parallels with other magazines which have followed the *Schooner,* but I do not consider that necessary to the present investigation. In Chapter 7 I have touched on several magazines contemporary with the *Schooner* in order to demonstrate how Nebraska's little magazine has functioned as part of a larger whole which has as its total purpose and effect the promotion of American writing.

In the other six chapters, I have concentrated on the *Schooner* itself, attempting to analyze it under significant divisions. Those divisions are, of course, arbitrary, and they overlap considerably. But, while perhaps less coherent than a chronological organization, such an analysis seems more likely to produce an understanding of what constitutes a little magazine. The information contained in these chapters has been derived almost entirely from primary sources: from the contents of the magazine's first twenty-five volumes, from more than two thousand letters, from the files of the campus newspaper, and from personal interviews with Dr. Wimberly and others familiar with various aspects of the magazine. Works of a secondary nature which have provided background information are listed in an appendix. Other appendixes give pertinent information concerning the *Schooner*'s contributors and staff members.

I have arbitrarily limited this study to the *Schooner*'s first twenty-five years, 1927 through 1951. Some limits had to be established, or the project could never have been completed; by the time information had been adjusted to accommodate the last issue of the magazine, a new issue would have appeared. The end of the first quarter of a century seemed an inviting terminal date. And, as a matter of fact, none of the general conclusions reached from the study of those years would require qualification in the light of the *Schooner*'s subsequent career.

I am deeply indebted to many people for their generous cooperation in making this book possible: to Professor Lowry C. Wimberly, who has kindly supplied much of the information here presented yet has never attempted to influence my appraisal of it; to his wife, Ida Boynton Wimberly, who through the years has preserved data which might otherwise have been lost, and who has collected such data for inclusion in this study; to Professor John T. Flanagan of the University of Illinois, upon whose experience and fine judgment I have drawn frequently and heavily; to Gene B. Hardy of the University of Nebraska, who was closer to this book during its composition than any other person except myself; to Arthur Heiserman, Stanley Moon, Miss Emily Schossberger, Frederick Christensen, Professor Wilbur Gaffney, and others at the University of Nebraska who have contributed in various ways toward the completion of this study. And finally, my deepest gratitude goes to my wife, without whose patience, understanding, and encouragement the project could never have been attempted.

PAUL R. STEWART

Butler University
May, 1955

CONTENTS

PREFACE   vii

1   *Background*   3

2   *The Beginnings*   21

3   *Financial History*   35

4   *Editorial Policy: Regionalism*   57

5   *Editorial Policy: Preferences and Prejudices*   79

6   *Submissions, Rejections and Contributors*   107

7   *The* Schooner *and Its Contemporaries*   139

8   *Achievements and Prospects*   165

APPENDIX   179

BIBLIOGRAPHY   199

THE *Prairie Schooner* STORY

1

Background

THE FIRST comprehensive study of the little magazine was published in 1946—*The Little Magazine,* by Frederick J. Hoffman, Charles Allen, and Carolyn F. Ulrich (Princeton University Press). The book constituted the American scholar's official recognition of what the American author had for some years realized, that the little magazine is a major force in modern literature. Indeed, the study finds in the little magazine the spawning ground for some eighty per cent of America's literary artists since 1912.

That year, 1912, marked the founding of Harriet Monroe's *Poetry: A Magazine of Verse,* which is probably the most famous and certainly one of the most influential of all American little magazines. A list of its early contributors, many of whom were first published by Miss Monroe, reads like a Who's Who of American Poetry. Because of *Poetry's* great impact upon American letters, the year of its founding is frequently taken as the date of origin of the modern little magazine. Perhaps one might as logically take the preceding year, 1911, which saw the founding of *The Masses, The Westminster Magazine,* and *Vision.* But any attempt to fix a date for the origin of the little magazine in America must be tentative and somewhat arbitrary. Long before either *The Masses* or *Poetry* first appeared, America had publications similar in many respects to the modern "little magazine," even if not customarily called by that name.

Hoffman has defined the little magazine as "a magazine designed to print artistic work which for reasons of commercial expediency is not acceptable to the money-minded periodicals or presses. . . . Little magazines are willing to lose money, to court ridicule, to ignore public tastes, willing to do almost anything—steal, beg, or undress in public—rather than sacrifice their right to print good material. . . ."[1]

Slightly over a century before that definition was written, America had a magazine which today might qualify under it. The *Dial,* an attractively printed quarterly of 136 pages, was founded in 1840 primarily to give the New England transcendentalists a voice which they could hardly have obtained from the commercial magazines appearing at the time. The statement of publication which appeared on the back cover of the first issue clearly anticipated the spirit of many little magazines originating some hundred years later:

> The purpose of this work is to furnish a medium for the freest expression of thought on the questions which interest earnest minds in every community. . . .
>
> Its contents will embrace a wide and varied range of subjects, and combining the characteristics of a Magazine and Review, it may present something both for those who read for instruction, and those who search for amusement.

[1] Frederick J. Hoffman *et al., The Little Magazine: A History and a Bibliography,* Princeton, 1946, p. 2.

Although it carried primarily essays and articles, the *Dial* printed a good number of poems. A total of twenty-three poems by Emerson appeared in the four volumes, and the *Dial* carried the work of several other poets, of whom Jones Very and the young Ellery Channing are perhaps the most significant. The first issue of the *Dial* contains a "discovery" equal in importance to any of which *Poetry* can boast, for in that issue appeared the first published prose of Henry David Thoreau. Other writers of note who contributed to the *Dial* included George Ripley, the elder William Ellery Channing, Bronson Alcott, Margaret Fuller, Caroline Sturgis, and Theodore Parker. And of course the *Dial* carried prose by Emerson, as well as his poetry.

The financial history of the *Dial* is clearly parallel to that of later American little magazines. When it first appeared, in July, 1840, its subscription list probably included fewer than one hundred names. Two years later, when Emerson replaced Margaret Fuller as editor, the circulation was about 220, and never in the two years of Emerson's editorship did it reach three hundred. The *Dial* did not attempt to pay contributors for their work, and, though it was originally proposed to pay Margaret Fuller a salary of two hundred dollars, it was unable to compensate its editors. Yet despite its low budget and its rather considerable subscription price of three dollars a year, the *Dial* cost Emerson "several hundred dollars" from his own pocket.[2]

The Massachusetts *Dial* had one immediate influence on the history of the little magazine. Its name was appropriated in 1880 for a literary review edited and published in Chicago by Francis F. Browne. The magazine, and the name, survived a change in ownership, a move to New York, and several changes in editorship, and in 1920 the New York *Dial,* edited

[2] George Willis Cooke, *An Historical and Biographical Introduction to The Dial,* Cleveland, 1902, I, 84-97.

by Scofield Thayer, became one of America's truly first-rate little magazines. But apart from that rather tenuous connection, the *Dial* of Emerson and Miss Fuller is not directly related to the more recent little magazines. It stands isolated by time from the little magazine movement, with nothing to parallel it in quality or design for several decades after its collapse in 1844.

The more immediate precursors of the modern little magazine began making their appearance toward the turn of the century. Two of the more significant were founded in 1895 a continent apart—*M'lle New York* and *The Lark. M'lle New York,* under the editorship of Vance Thompson and, for a time, James G. Huneker, was a "gay, satirical, comical" fortnightly review of an announced rebel nature; its statement of publication read: "M'lle New York is not concerned with the public. Her only ambition is to disintegrate some small portion of the public into its original component parts—the aristocracies of birth, wit, learning and art and the joyously vulgar mob."[3] Meanwhile in San Francisco, Gelett Burgess was writing, editing, and illustrating his sixteen-page *Lark.* The magazine had an immediate appeal and had begun to make money when Burgess abandoned it to move east in 1896. It carried essays, fiction, and poetry. Probably the best known item which Burgess published is his quatrain about the purple cow, which was written for the first issue.[4]

The predecessors of the little magazine, however, were not restricted to America's coasts. Some of the most vigorous of the literary magazines to appear around the turn of the century emanated from the Midlands.

A truly sparkling miscellany was Herbert Stuart Stone's *Chap-Book,* published in Chicago from May, 1894, to July,

---

[3] Hoffman, *op. cit.,* p. 236.
[4] C. H. Towne, "The One-Man Magazines," *American Mercury,* LXIII, 104-108 (July, 1946).

1898. A small semi-monthly, the *Chap-Book* was attractively printed and smartly illustrated. Its chief distinction, however, was the quality of its contributions. Among its contributors were Henry James, Stephen Crane, W. B. Yeats, Robert Louis Stevenson, Eugene Field, Max Beerbohm, H. G. Wells, Julian Hawthorne, William Vaughan Moody, Bliss Carman, George E. Woodberry, E. C. Stedman, Hamlin Garland, and Thomas Hardy. It was not, then, strictly a regional venture; it drew to Chicago manuscripts from the cultural centers of the United States and even from across the sea.

Less excellent, perhaps, but equally important in preparing the way for the little magazines of the twentieth century were a group of periodicals which sprang up in the less populous areas of the Midwest. One purpose, and achievement, of the little magazine movement has been the decentralization of the nation's culture. This decentralization had begun before 1900, with the aid of magazines which appeared closely behind the advancing frontier. Some of the magazines were as crude and primitive as early life in the region, and most of them were far from literary. The majority of them were collections of miscellaneous informative articles dealing with subjects of special interest to the farmer and plainsman.[5] But a few of them attempted to be literary, and a very few were sufficiently successful to merit attention.

One of the earliest of such magazines was the *Literary Northwest*, edited by Mary H. Severance and H. T. Carpenter, which originated in St. Paul, Minnesota, in March, 1892. It followed several earlier Minnesota magazines dating back as far as 1830, all of which were primarily journalistic and none of which achieved any genuine success. The *Literary Northwest* was distinguished from those earlier attempts in that it had literary pretensions. Instead of devoting all its space to ex-

---

[5] See John T. Flanagan, "Early Literary Periodicals in Minnesota," *Minnesota History*, XXVI, 293-311 (December, 1945).

pository treatment of immediate and practical problems, it
sought and achieved a balance of fiction, sketches, verse,
articles, reviews and editorial comment. It drew almost entirely from local or nearby contributors. One of its more noteworthy offerings was a segment of Hamlin Garland's novel
Jason Edwards. As an attempt the *Literary Northwest* was
significant, even though as an achievement it was inferior to
many other magazines that were to follow. John T. Flanagan,
in appraising it, remarks that it "was not good enough to survive. Its verse was brief and trite and its fiction flabbily sentimental, but its articles were usually clear and vigorous . . .
and both its literary criticism and its reviews were commenda-
ble."[6]

The *Literary Northwest* succumbed after the issue for July,
1893, and was absorbed by another non-metropolitan publication of the hinterlands which proved much more successful—
Johnson Brigham's *Midland Monthly*, of Des Moines, Iowa.
The rather impressive first issue of Brigham's *Midland,* dated
January, 1894, carried contributions from Hamlin Garland and
Alice French (who as Octave Thanet was soon to become well
known for her short stories). The magazine led a vigorous
existence for five and a half years; it absorbed, in addition to
the *Literary Northwest,* three other publications: *Tainter's
Magazine, New Bohemia,* and *Illustrated Iowa.* With the aid
of subscription drives which offered such premiums as books,
encyclopedias, and cameras, Brigham built his circulation to
a peak of thirteen thousand.[7]

In the size of its circulation and the methods used to
achieve it, the *Midland Monthly* hardly resembled the later
little magazines. But in other important respects it clearly
anticipated such magazines. Brigham attempted to maintain

---

[6] *Ibid.,* pp. 300-303.
[7] For the information in this and the following paragraphs concerning
the *Midland Monthly,* I am indebted to Louella M. Wright, "*The Midland
Monthly,*" *Iowa Journal of History and Politics,* XLV, 3-61 (January, 1947).

a high quality in his magazine, and his emphasis was consistently on the literary and cultural. The *Midland* carried many articles, but they dealt with subjects of general interest to the educated reader: travel, history, biography, social studies, education. And considerable space was devoted to the purely creative; the *Midland* carried an average of seventy-five short stories a year and about fifty poems. It also made good use of artistic illustrations and sketches.

But the most significant aspect of the *Midland Monthly*, to one interested in the later little magazines, is its editorial policy or, more specifically, the motives which prompted Brigham to found it and which governed his selection of material. In these respects the *Midland Monthly* was the direct predecessor of such later little magazines as John T. Frederick's *Midland*, Harold G. Merriam's *Frontier*, and Lowry C. Wimberly's *Prairie Schooner*.

Brigham was devoted to the Midwest, and he founded his magazine primarily as a spokesman for that region. He felt that the area was beginning to mature, culturally and artistically, and hoped through the pages of the *Midland* to provide an audience for those midwestern writers whose potential talents were being ignored by eastern publishers. He encouraged the unknown midwestern writer to develop his skill. Toward that end, he offered quarterly prizes for writing, announcing in an editorial column that he wished to open the *Midland* to those who, though possessed of talent, had not yet acquired all the "details of professional literary work and the prestige of assured position in the literary world."[8] As a result of this conscious appeal to writers from the region, by far the majority of the *Midland*'s contributors came from Iowa, and most of the rest were from neighboring states. Few of their names would be recognized today—perhaps Brigham's optimism was a few years premature. Nevertheless, Brigham did

---

[8] *Midland Monthly*, I, 615, quoted by Wright, *op. cit.*, p. 35.

stimulate an awareness of literature and did help establish a literary tradition in the Midwest.

Coupled with Brigham's interest in the midwestern writer was his advocacy of realism or, as he and Hamlin Garland chose to call it, "veritism"—the unadorned, unsentimental presentation of environment and situation as they are observed. With that as one of his chief editorial convictions, it followed that the contributions which Brigham chose to print were mostly those which portrayed the region. There is a strong regional theme in most of the fiction, and the poetry is largely of the type known as "local color," frequently making use of dialect. In an editorial for the issue of July, 1895, Brigham proclaimed the *Midland* to be "peculiarly the historian and the prophet of this wide new land which is so rapidly reaching out toward art and the finer things of life and the greater things of human achievement."[9]

Before he abandoned his magazine, Brigham had the satisfaction of seeing results from his attempt to bring the culture of the plains to the attention of the nation's population centers. The *Midland* was noted and praised in the pages of such publications as the New York *Tribune,* the New York *World,* the Boston *Herald,* the Washington (D. C.) *Press,* and the San Francisco *Post.*

Of equal importance in the establishment of a midwestern culture was William C. Edgar's *Bellman,* which appeared in Minneapolis in 1906 and continued until 1919. Like the *Midland Monthly,* Edgar's magazine was too commercial to be properly called a little magazine. It was more nearly an imitation of the eastern quality magazines than a true ancestor of the non-commercial journals of small circulation which were soon to appear. The magazine was founded under a capital structure of twenty-five thousand dollars. Before the first issue appeared, Edgar helped insure the financial success of the

[9] Quoted in Wright, *op. cit.,* p. 15.

Bellman by a thorough canvass for subscriptions and advertising. From that time until it discontinued publication, the magazine was never in serious financial difficulty. During its thirteen years, its receipts totaled $457,000, obtained largely from advertisers, and its expenditures totaled $427,000, of which $95,000 went to contributors and $32,000 for art work. At the time of its last issue, the *Bellman* was able to make full refund for unfilled subscriptions, without draining its treasury.[10]

Yet despite the financial success of the *Bellman*, Edgar's primary interest was consistently literary rather than commercial. He undertook his venture partly because he was dissatisfied with the quality of the magazines being offered the American public at the time and felt that a magazine of high literary aspirations was needed. In the tenth anniversary number of the *Bellman* (July 1, 1916, p. 15), Edgar summarized the views which had directed his efforts:

> The assumption was that, while the mass of people might be too busy, or too careless, or too rudimentary in their approach, to distinguish between a publication with high editorial, literary, and typographical standards, there were in existence a sufficient number of discriminating persons to realize the difference, and, given time and the earnest of consistent effort in this direction, they would respond cheerfully to the attempt with the necessary support, in both subscriptions and advertising, to make it worth while.

He also indicated why, although he might have founded his magazine in the East, he deliberately had chosen to publish it in Minnesota:

[10] William C. Edgar, editorial in the *Bellman*, XXVI, 705-707 (June 28, 1919). See also Flanagan, *op. cit.,* pp. 307-311. The figure of $32,000 for art work is an estimate derived from Edgar's statement (XX, 23) that during the *Bellman's* first ten years he expended $25,000 for that purpose.

The Northwest was obviously a better field to start in than the East; first, because the editorial and mechanical machinery was at hand and the necessary capital could be secured without great effort; second, because, in proportion to the population, it contained a larger percentage of people in whom the true American spirit still dominated; third, because the East had a plethora of publications, good, bad or indifferent, while, apart from its daily newspapers and trade journals, the Northwest had practically none. Finally, because the distinction to be obtained in issuing such a periodical from a place where, according to accepted notions, it could not possibly exist, except as an exotic, promised to be greater when recognition finally came, and, viewed merely as a sporting proposition the idea was inviting.

Like Brigham's *Midland*, the *Bellman* carried more reviews and articles than fiction, and the articles covered a wide range of subjects. Despite its weekly appearance, it published only about fifty poems a year, and only thirty or forty short stories. By far the majority of the contributions came from regular members of the staff or were solicited from regular contributors; the *Bellman* carried only about two unsolicited contributions each week.[11] Yet it received about 43,000 such manuscripts during its thirteen years, and during its last year it was receiving them at the rate of sixty-five a day.[12]

In selecting from those many manuscripts, the only criterion which Edgar consciously applied was that of quality. He did not, as Brigham had done, concentrate on printing the works of previously unpublished writers, nor did he deliberately choose those manuscripts signed by familiar names. He avowed in his farewell issue that the *Bellman* (which Edgar consistently personalized with the masculine pronoun) "has

[11] *Cf.* the *Little Review*, which, according to its editor, Margaret Anderson, in all its years published only two or three unsolicited manuscripts. (*Little Review Anthology*, New York, 1953, p. 21.)

[12] Edgar, editorial in the *Bellman*, XXVI, 706 (June 28, 1919).

always made his selections honestly and sincerely, not influenced by the names of writers or their reputations, but desirous of choosing whatever was best of the material sent him."[13]

Edgar's principle of selection brought to the pages of the *Bellman* much material of real worth. Among its contributors one finds the names of Richard Burton, Carl Becker, Hardin Craig, Louis Untermeyer, Alfred Noyes, Joyce Kilmer, Hilaire Belloc, Arthur Quiller-Couch, Sara Teasdale, Christopher Morley, Carl Van Vechten, Stephen Leacock, Arthur Symonds, John Hall Wheelock, Witter Bynner, Bliss Carman, Ben Ames Williams, and Oscar Williams. The articles and reviews were generally cultural in their emphasis and competent in their style. The poetry and fiction, though limited in quantity, were of a quality to establish the *Bellman* as one of the leading periodicals of its day. The Boston *Transcript,* which annually surveyed the nation's periodicals and evaluated their literary contents, consistently assigned the *Bellman* high ratings in both poetry and fiction. The *Transcript* for January 8, 1916, reviewing the short stories of the past year, paid the *Bellman* the following tribute:

> The Bellman is remarkable for the brilliance and power of its fiction. The averages this year show clearly that its percentage of distinctive stories is nearly double that of the American weekly which most nearly approaches it. The quality of the Bellman's poetry is a matter of national knowledge. It is fully equalled by the Bellman's fiction, which renders it one of the three or four American periodicals necessary to every student of our spiritual history.[14]

The final number of the *Bellman* (June 28, 1919) is devoted almost entirely to editorial reflections over the career

---

[13] *Ibid.*
[14] Quoted in the *Bellman,* XX, 447 (April 15, 1916).

which the issue concluded. In that number the dominant tone is one of quiet pride in the *Bellman*'s achievements and gratitude for the justification of Edgar's belief in the existence of an intelligent reading public. Edgar indicated that neither a lack of readers nor a lack of funds was responsible for the discontinuance of his magazine. On the contrary, "the Bellman has chosen, he thinks wisely, to make his bow while yet his friendly audience is in the humor to urge him to continue."

But despite its apparent vitality, the *Bellman* was by 1919 something of an anachronism. It was a commercial miscellany which had managed to survive into an age dominated culturally by the non-commercial little magazine. The change came during the second decade of the century. In his bibliography, Hoffman lists more than fifty American little magazines which had their origin during the ten years beginning with 1911. During those years, the commercial "quality" magazines were losing their vitality as literary media. In surveying the period, Malcolm Cowley has pointed out:

> In 1910 [*Harper's, Scribner's* and the *Century*] still had a combined circulation of more than 500,000, but they lost half their readers during the next ten years. The *Atlantic* proved to be more flexible; it surrendered some of its literary standing and found a new public; and *Harper's* after 1920 followed a similar course.[15]

Cowley attributes the change in the American publishing scene to "a gulf between the tastes of the broad public and the aims of serious writers." The explanation is a plausible one; it agrees essentially with Hoffman's suggestion that the little magazines of the 1910's were "consciously established to promote a regenerative literature. Little magazine editors knew

---

[15] Malcolm Cowley, "Magazine Business: 1910-46," *The New Republic,* CXV, 521 (October 21, 1946). Both *Scribner's* and the *Century* ceased publication in 1930.

that there were already writers such as Robinson, Masters, Sara Teasdale, poets with much to say provided they could find a place to publish consistently. And the editors suspected that there were many unknowns who could be encouraged to write if they were offered a fair chance of publication."[16]

Regardless of the reason, the fact is certain: beginning in 1911 or 1912 the responsibility for discovering and encouraging the nation's writers, as well as the privilege of printing the best of the nation's literature, came increasingly to rest upon the growing group of American little magazines.

Among the most vigorous of the early little magazines, and of special interest to the present study, was one established by John T. Frederick in Iowa City, in January, 1915. Frederick gave his magazine the name formerly used by Johnson Brigham, the *Midland*. It was an appropriate choice, for in many ways Frederick's magazine was the direct lineal descendant of such midwestern magazines as the *Literary Northwest*, the *Midland Monthly*, and the *Bellman*. It proved, indeed, to be a culmination of those earlier attempts to establish a significant literary voice in the plains region.

The *Midland* survived for over eighteen years, longer than any of the commercial magazines previously discussed and far longer than the average modern little magazine. Its home during those years was never very permanent. Born on the campus of the University of Iowa, it followed Frederick in 1917 to the State Teachers' College in Moorhead, Minnesota; in 1919 to a farm in Glennie, Michigan; in 1921 back to Iowa City; in 1923 to the University of Pittsburgh; in 1924 back again to Iowa City; and finally in 1930 to Chicago, where it died a victim of the depression in 1933. Through most of that career the *Midland* appeared monthly; for three short periods it became a bimonthly, and during 1925 it appeared semimonthly. In format and page size it underwent several changes

---

[16] Hoffman, *op. cit.*, p. 7.

during its eighteen years. As a monthly it customarily carried some thirty pages, but financial pressures frequently reduced its size; one issue in 1923 carried only one contribution, and another printed only two poems. The magazine was never a success financially. It carried no advertising. Apart from a few "sustaining subscriptions" it depended entirely upon sales for its income. And through most of its life the *Midland* had a circulation of less than five hundred. Frederick was forced personally to absorb an annual deficit, and when that deficit became prohibitive, publication was finally suspended.[17]

Though it was never very stable physically or financially, the *Midland* was in other important respects firm and unswerving. Frederick consistently placed literary quality above all other considerations in selecting manuscripts for his magazine. He firmly resisted the temptation to "go commercial" and sacrifice some of his editorial independence to greater financial security. His views are expressed frequently in the editorial pages of the *Midland,* but perhaps nowhere more succinctly than in an editorial addressed "To the New Reader," which appeared at the beginning of the *Midland*'s eighth year (January, 1922, p. 37):

> The *Midland* believes in the opportunity and the necessity for sincere artistic achievement in contemporary American life. It seeks to encourage such achievement, especially in the art of writing and especially in the middle west, by bringing worthy fiction, poetry, and essays, in fitting form, to the attention of sympathetic and discerning readers. In the second place, the *Midland* is not commercial. Its editor believes that a literary magazine, like a church or a school, should be governed by other considerations than those of profit. Accordingly every cent of income from the seven years of the *Midland*'s existence has been devoted to the actual

---

[17] See Lois T. Hartley, "The *Midland*," *Iowa Journal of History,* **XLVII,** 325-344 (October, 1949) and Hoffman, *op. cit.,* pp. 140-147.

expense of printing and mailing the magazine. The *Mid-land* pays no salaries, nor does it pay for manuscripts. . . . It is pledged to remain uncommercial. No one will ever "make money" from the *Midland.*

From the *Midland*'s first issue, Frederick regarded his magazine as a refuge for the middlewestern writer, who he felt was being unjustly ignored by the eastern publishers. The magazine bore the subtitle "A Magazine of the Middle West" from its founding until it moved to Chicago in 1930 to become "A National Magazine." Even in that move Frederick sought a larger base of operations from which more effectively to combat what he regarded as the "literary despotism" of the eastern press.[18] In that respect, Frederick was consistently a champion of the Midwest. And in its early contributors, the themes of much of its fiction, and the subjects of many reviews and articles, the *Midland* reflects the place of its origin. It is therefore generally termed a "regional" magazine.

Yet, as Frederick has suggested,[19] the *Midland* was perhaps no more regional than many other little magazines whose proper region happened to be New England or New York; its regionalism was simply more apparent because of its relative isolation. Certainly neither the contents of the magazine nor its list of contributors reflects the blind and narrow sort of regionalism which might be termed provincialism. Frederick gave space freely to manuscripts from other sections of the country when such contributions were available to him, and once the *Midland* was firmly established, an increasing number of its contributors came from outside the Midwest. Before its collapse it had become truly "A National Magazine," and despite its small circulation it was held in national respect.

---

[18] The *Midland,* XVI, 369-371 (November-December, 1930).
[19] *Ibid.,* VI, 1-2 (January-February-March, 1920).

One thing which has served to magnify the importance of the *Midland* is the fact that it seemed to establish a tradition which has been followed by several other little magazines. Among later magazines which not only are commonly called regional but which also resemble the *Midland* in having originated on college campuses and in having printed a balanced selection of fiction, poetry, articles, and essays, one finds the *Southwest Review,* the *New Mexico Quarterly,* the *Frontier,* the *Rocky Mountain Review* (later the *Western Review*), the *University of Kansas City Review,* and the subject of the present study, the *Prairie Schooner.*

During the years 1911 through 1926, some 134 little magazines were founded in America. During the same years, one hundred of those magazines died. There were, then, thirty-four American little magazines at the end of 1926.[20] The magazines constituted a heterogeneous group. Many of them were being published in the nation's population centers, but a few emanated from such little known spots as Platter, Oklahoma (the *Poet's Scroll*) or Larned, Kansas (the *Harp*). Nineteen of the magazines were completely or almost completely restricted to the publication of poetry; four carried only essays and articles; none printed prose fiction exclusively; eleven published some combination of the three forms. Some spoke for a region (the *Midland,* the *Frontier*) or a political school (the *Modern Quarterly,* the *New Masses*); others were essentially the expression of a single personality (the *Country Bard,* the *Circle*). The magazines differed in size, in frequency, in quality, and in vitality.

Among these magazines, indeed, there were more points of difference than of similarity. The only significant common denominators—and it is by these that the little magazine is today commonly identified—were (1) their interest in good but

---

[20] Hoffman, *op. cit.,* pp. 240-283. Hoffman's definition of the little magazine has been followed throughout.

unsaleable literature, and (2) the precariousness of their existence. Most of them had crept into this world meager and unannounced; most of them would creep out the same way. More than half of them would perish within a decade.

The huge crop of little magazines which blossomed during the first two decades of the century might suggest that the little magazine springs up spontaneously, or grows "volunteer" like the dandelion or sunflower. That may have been the case with some of the little magazines which bore one or two bright blossoms and then died. But it was not the case with such perennials as Harriet Monroe's *Poetry* or Frederick's *Midland*. Nor was it the case with the *Prairie Schooner*. The growth of such a magazine involves dropping the proper seed in a fertile soil, giving it a great deal of cultivation, securing the blessings of fate, and then hoping that the seed will bear fruit.

2

The Beginnings

By 1926, men like Johnson Brigham, William Edgar, and
John T. Frederick had confirmed the existence in the Midwest of soil favorable to the growth of literary magazines.
And Lincoln, Nebraska, was probably as fertile a spot as Des
Moines, Minneapolis, or Iowa City. Although it had a population of only about 65,000, Lincoln was the center of trade
and culture for a considerable area of the state. In addition
to being the state capital, it contained six other state institu-
tions. It boasted five movie and vaudeville houses, two legitimate theaters, and four schools of higher education.

The University of Nebraska was, in 1926, the cultural
heart of Lincoln. Although perhaps most famous for its powerful football teams, the school was also the scene of some artistic activity. It had its own concert orchestra and chorus, an
active dramatics group, and a growing collection of paintings,
which was open to the public. And each year, in the large
Coliseum, it scheduled a series of musical concerts which
brought to Lincoln individual artists and occasionally entire
orchestras or operatic companies from the East.

Despite the university's relative isolation from the American literary centers, there was on the campus considerable

interest in literature. Memories of Willa Cather, Dorothy
Canfield, and Edwin Ford Piper, all Nebraska products who
had succeeded as writers, contributed to that interest. But
of more immediate importance was the presence of a flourish-
ing College of Arts and Sciences and, in that college, an active
department of English.[1] The university catalogue for 1926-
1927 describes among the offerings of the department of English eleven courses in philology, twenty-seven courses in composition above the freshman level, and fifty-five courses in
literature. A surprising number of these courses reflected an
interest in modern literature and its techniques. The program
in composition included, for example, courses in narrative
techniques, a course devoted entirely to the short story, and
a two-semester sequence in poetics. Among the literature
courses were two in modern prose, two in contemporary drama
and fiction, and a graduate seminar in "present literary forms
and tendencies."

But perhaps even more significant than the course offerings in stimulating a general interest in literature was the
presence on the Nebraska faculty of several people whose personal interest in literature was so vital as to be easily com-
municated to the students. There was Prosser Hall Frye, whose
criticism had established him as an authority on Greek tragedy and a leader of the neo-humanist school, and there was
Frye's younger devotee, Sherlock B. Gass, who in addition to
his critical work had published two volumes of informal essays. The chairman of the department of English, Lucius A.
Sherman, had published five books on literary form and three
studies of Shakespeare, in addition to poetic translations from
the Norwegian. J. E. LeRossignol, Dean of the College of
Business Administration, had written a novel and several

[1] There was, in the year 1926-1927, a total of 5,782 resident students at
the Lincoln city campus. Of this number, some 38 per cent were enrolled
in the College of Arts and Sciences. The largest single departments among
the seventeen in that college were those of Fine Arts, Romance Languages,
and English.

short stories of the French-Canadian frontier. Hartley Burr Alexander, chairman of the department of philosophy, was the author of two books of criticism, a book of essays, several plays and pageants, two volumes of poetry, and many other poems published but not collected. He was also active as an associate editor of the *Midland* magazine, which position he had held since the *Midland*'s first appearance.

The combined effect of a recognized literary tradition, a strong program of courses, and the presence in high places of literary practitioners as well as critics, was to create on the campus an atmosphere characterized by an interest in literature not just as a historical phenomenon but as something still alive, still capable of being produced.

A part of this literary atmosphere, and a product of it, was the small group of men which was chartered, on October 26, 1926, as the Wordsmith chapter of Sigma Upsilon, "national honorary literary fraternity." The group, consisting primarily of students but including Assistant Professor Lowry C. Wimberly of the English department, had been meeting unofficially for some time before the issuance of the charter. Its main business was the discussion of literature; it served no political or professional ends. It was not even recognized in the university catalogue's list of societies. But this group, which might well have passed unnoticed, became suddenly important when it decided to sponsor a campus literary magazine.

The suggestion for such a magazine came early in 1926 from V. Royce West, a member of the fraternity and a senior in the College of Arts and Sciences.[2] He presented the idea

---

[2] The *Prairie Schooner*, XII, 230 (Fall, 1938). Henceforth references to the *Schooner* will be indicated in the text by issue, year, and page, thus: (Fall, 1938, 250). This method of designation has been chosen in preference to volume and issue numbers because, while identifying as exactly, it gives a better idea of chronology. Through Volume IX (1935) the first issue of each year is called the "Winter" number; after that, it is called the "Spring" number.

to Dr. Wimberly, and the two had little trouble in generating enthusiasm among other members of the fraternity. Several of those members were motivated in part by personal interests. They had ambitions to write and to publish their writings. They knew the difficulty experienced by the unknown midwestern writer who tried to publish in the established magazines of the East, and they welcomed the idea of a magazine specifically designed to carry their literary creations. In addition, a sense of local pride operated to make the idea of a campus magazine attractive. The members of the fraternity had access, through the university library, to several little magazines including the *Midland,* the *Frontier,* and the *Southwest Review,* each of which was published on a university campus far from the nation's publishing centers. And the members felt that there were, on and about the Nebraska campus, both adequate material and sufficient interest to sustain a magazine similar in quality and scope to those other successful campus magazines.[3]

Wimberly, as the only faculty member of Sigma Upsilon, was elected "chairman of the board of editors." Fortunately for the project, his qualifications included much more than his academic position.

Although not quite thirty-six, Wimberly had already acquired, in addition to his Ph.D. degree, wide experience. Born in the Mississippi River town of Plaquemine, Louisiana, on Christmas day, 1890, Wimberly had spent most of his adolescence and young manhood in the Midwest. Before beginning his academic training he worked in a variety of jobs; he was a bookkeeper in a Colorado sugar factory, a clerk and general handyman in a small Nebraska hotel, a farmhand and

---

[3] This information and, throughout the study, other information not the subject of written records has been obtained through personal conversation with Dr. Wimberly, who has read such passages and affirmed their accuracy. See also Emily Heine, "Ripe Old Age of 25," Omaha *Sunday World-Herald Magazine,* June 24, 1951, p. 5.

physician's stenographer in Iowa. Lured by a father and five older brothers, all of whom were ordained Presbyterian ministers, he contemplated entering the ministry and did actually preach one Sunday sermon, after which he decided that his interests lay in other directions.

Wimberly's capacity for hard work is indicated not only by the variety of jobs he held, but by the manner in which he acquired his education. In February, 1910, he married Ida May Boynton, and the following year he entered the University of Nebraska as a freshman majoring in English literature. With the cooperation of his wife, who was sufficiently interested in his career to make the necessary sacrifices, he earned three degrees in the next fourteen years, despite the increasing obligations of a growing family. By the time he received his A.B. degree in 1916, he was the father of two children. He was appointed an instructor in English, and while teaching full time he pursued his graduate studies, receiving an A.M. degree in 1920 and a Ph.D. (with a promotion to an assistant professorship) in 1925. By that time his children numbered four.

The tremendous energy indicated by that successful struggle for an education was (and is) partially concealed behind an appearance of deliberateness and nonchalance. Wimberly's drawling speech may reflect his southern origin, and his slow, deliberate movement may be the effect of the malaria which he contracted in Louisiana as a boy and carried for fifteen years. But his casual manner is something more than a physical habit; it stems from an equanimity approaching nervelessness, which has enabled him to remain calm in times of crisis and avoid those ulcers which the pressure of work might have caused in a person of less composure. Allied with this equanimity is a keen sense of humor. Though seldom moved to audible laughter, he smiles easily, and his speech, whether in casual conversation or in the classroom, is enlivened by a crackling wit always dry and frequently ironic but seldom malicious. He has an almost sentimental sympathy for the underdog, which has ideally fitted him for dealing with the unsuccessful and frequently discouraged authors who submit manuscripts to the editor of the little magazine.

But Wimberly's most important qualification for his new position as editor was, of course, his knowledge of what constitutes good writing. It was a qualification as yet largely unproved in 1926. His own writing for publication had been restricted to two monographs, five scholarly articles, a few poems, and one short story. He had co-edited an anthology of essays. Apart from that, the only editing he had done had been that of student compositions written for his courses in English.

Since the founding of the *Schooner,* however, he has amply demonstrated his abilities. His own writing, though quantitatively limited by his many other duties, has found a ready market, has been frequently reprinted, and has been praised by such critics as Edward J. O'Brien and H. L. Mencken. Since 1926 he has written one book, collaborated on another, and either edited or helped to edit five more.[4] And the *Prairie*

---

[4] A complete bibliography of Wimberly's publications, prepared by Mrs. Wimberly, includes the following items:

Stories: twenty, published in *Sunshine Magazine,* the *Prairie Schooner, American Mercury, Forum, Harper's, Windsor Quarterly, Yale Review, Western Review.* Reprints in *English Argosy, Town Talk, Main Street, Best Short Stories of 1931, Short Story Hits of 1933, Short Story Hits of 1932, Short Stories of Today* (1934), *American Writing 1944.*

Articles: thirty-five, published in *Poet Lore, American Speech, Englische Studien, American Mercury, Frontier-Midland, Prairie Schooner, Atlantic Monthly, Nebraska Alumnus, Book Week, University of Kansas City Review, Eleusis of Chi Omega, Awgwan, Town Talk, Dictionary of World Literature.* Reprints in *The Pocket Atlantic, Magazine Digest, Digest and Review, Better English.*

Books: author of *Ministrelsy, Music, and the Dance in English and Scottish Popular Ballads* (University of Nebraska, 1921), *Death and Burial Lore in English and Scottish Popular Ballads* (University of Nebraska, 1927), *Folklore in the English and Scottish Ballads* (University of Chicago, 1928) ; co-author of *Using Better English* (New York, 1937); editor of *The Famous Cats of Fairyland* (New York, 1938), *Prairie Schooner Caravan* (University of Nebraska, 1943), *Mid Country* (University of

Schooner testifies to his ability at criticizing and editing the writing of others. His election to the post of "chairman of the board of editors" was, then, a happy choice.

The other four members of the fraternity elected to the new editorial staff were all students: Roscoe Schaupp, Jacob Gable, Marion Edward Stanley, and Volta Torrey. Royce West, who had conceived the idea of founding the magazine, took over the duties of business manager. That these five students were unusually capable and well adapted to their positions on the *Schooner* staff is suggested by their careers subsequent to graduation. Schaupp became a professor of English at Ohio State University. Gable is editor of the trade magazine *Writer's Markets and Methods*. Stanley, after serving as head of the Associated Press London bureau and executive editor of *Esquire-Coronet* magazines, became a successful novelist. Torrey is the editor of *Popular Science* magazine. West served for a time as editor of the *Nebraska Alumnus* magazine, then entered a career in business and advertising; he is now publicity director for the Pillsbury Mills, in Minneapolis.

The newly constituted staff of the *Schooner,* realizing that many student ventures fail for the lack of faculty support, undertook as its first task the making of some influential friends. Wimberly explained the projected magazine to Professor Sherman, head of the English department, and with little effort persuaded him to serve on an "advisory board." As the second member of that two-man board the staff secured R. D. Scott, director of freshman English, who like Sherman was almost immediately sympathetic toward the project. A delegation from the fraternity approached Professor Hartley Burr Alexander, whose chairmanship in philosophy, experience as an author, and work with the *Midland* constituted a

Nebraska, 1945) ; co-editor of *Essays on Agriculture* (New York, 1921) , *Ideas and Models* (New York, 1935), *Dominant Types in British and American Literature* (New York, 1949).

triple recommendation. Alexander offered encouragement and suggested a possible name for the new magazine. The editors cheerfully accepted the encouragement but rejected the name "Hesperides" as too classic and high-flown to fit the magazine which they hoped to produce.

The biggest chore during those months of preparing the magazine was the collecting of material for an impressive first issue. Once a magazine has become an established literary market, the editor selects its contents from the morning mail, but securing contributions for a magazine not yet in existence presents problems in salesmanship and public relations as well as in criticism and selection. Some of the material came from members of the fraternity: two poems by Marion Stanley, a sketch by Volta Torrey, and a review by Roscoe Schaupp. Most of the contributions were obtained (often with the aid of friendly teachers of composition) from the student body; these included an excellent lead story, "The Vine," by Marie Macumber, who had won honorable mention in *Harper*'s intercollegiate contest for 1926 and who, as Mari Sandoz, was later to write several successful books including *Old Jules,* winner of the 1935 *Atlantic Monthly*-Little, Brown $5,000 award.

Some manuscripts for the first issue came from the university faculty and staff. The editors obtained a poem from Martin S. Peterson, instructor in English, a satire from Zora Schaupp of the philosophy department, two poems from the librarian Gilbert H. Doane, and an essay from the assistant librarian Nellie Jane Compton. To secure for the first issue some high-level name appeal they also obtained a review from Professor Sherman and—what was for advertising purposes the *pièce de résistance*—an autobiographical sketch by Lincoln's Bess Streeter Aldrich, whose best-sellers about pioneer days had made her name a household word in the local region.

The final selection of manuscripts for the first issue presented a wide variety of literary types. There were four short stories, twelve poems, three essays, two reviews, two prose sketches, and a play.

While the manuscripts for the first issue were being collected, the editors puzzled over a name for their magazine. Wimberly's first suggestion, "The Covered Wagon," met with general approval and prevailed until he amended it to "The Prairie Schooner." The name seemed admirably suited: it was unique, it had the regional tone which the editors hoped to impart to their magazine, and it was simple and pleasant sounding. Wimberly secured from Ben Albert Benson, instructor in drawing and painting, a cover design (two and a half by three inches) of a pioneer walking beside a prairie schooner drawn by two oxen.

By November, 1926, the magazine had taken shape. Its staff, its title, its tone, its appearance, and most of the contents of its first issue had been determined. The campus newspaper *Daily Nebraskan* carried, on November 10, a full-column front page story announcing the magazine's approaching publication: "The Prairie Schooner, a literary quarterly to be published by the Nebraska Chapter of Sigma Upsilon, national literary fraternity, will appear December first, and at three month intervals thereafter." The article went on to describe, in considerable detail, the first issue of the magazine as it finally appeared.

But the announcement of the publication date as December 1 was premature. There remained for the staff the inescapable problem of financing the first issue.

Thus far the editors had managed to operate on a budget of nothing at all. It had early been decided that the magazine would not attempt to pay either contributors or staff members. And because the *Schooner* had used Wimberly's office as a base of operations, there had been no expenditure for a physical plant. Nor were the editors worried about immediate distribution costs; as the circulation of the first issue would be entirely local, the distribution could be accomplished through the legwork of the unpaid staff members. There was one inescapable expense, however—that of getting the magazine in print. Three hundred copies of a well printed, well bound magazine of about a hundred pages would cost, West discovered, about $250, that sum to include the paper, the printing, and the binding. It was hoped that the *Schooner*, once under way, would become self-supporting; but before it could become a reality, the editors had to obtain $250 from somewhere. The fraternity had no funds of its own, nor did any of its members have cash to invest in the project.

It was in this very first crisis that the value of the right friends was demonstrated. Professor Sherman, a ranking dean and departmental chairman with forty-four years' service in the university, had considerable influence with the university administration. He succeeded in procuring, even though the magazine was not an official university publication, a subsidy to cover the costs of the first number of the *Prairie Schooner*. West made arrangements with Ralph D. Scott of the university printing department to handle the printing and binding, and the *Prairie Schooner* became a reality.

The first issue, dated "January, 1927" appeared on January 12. It was neat but inconspicuous; its dull yellow cover carried in plain black type the title, the small cut designed by Benson, the date January, 1927, and "Volume I, Number 1." The ninety-two pages were well printed on high-quality paper. Inside, page 1 bore the following notice of publication:

> The *Prairie Schooner* is an outlet for literary work in the University of Nebraska and a medium for publication of the finest writing of the prairie country. It is sponsored by the Wordsmith Chapter of Sigma Upsilon, a national literary fraternity, and is published with the aid of the University of Nebraska. The present number marks the first issue of this quarterly.
>
> If there is sufficient interest in the publication, the publishers will continue the issuance. Immediate subscriptions will largely indicate the interest in the

venture and will determine the fate of the magazine. This is a non-commercial venture. Income is dependent upon subscriptions, advertising, and donations.

Those persons who are sufficiently interested in the publication to subsidize it by donations are urged to do so immediately. Notice of the subscription and strict accounting for its use will be given.

The second issue will appear April 1, 1927.

The last page of the issue carried two forms, one for placing subscriptions at $1.50 a year and the other to accompany direct financial contributions. The entire press run of this first issue, three hundred copies, was disposed of by direct sale at forty cents a copy, primarily on the campus but also on downtown newsstands.

Immediate campus reception of the *Prairie Schooner* appears to have been generally favorable. The *Daily Nebraskan* carried on January 14 the following article:

> The Prairie Schooner, a speck on the campus literary horizon for the past few weeks, has at last taken definite form and copies are being distributed from leading news stands of the city. This magazine, an innovation at the University of Nebraska, is a publication well worthy of the highest praise, and its staff members are to be commended for the manner in which they have prepared the first issue. . . .
>
> It may be possible that the reports calling the publication one of high literary quality will cause the average reader to think that it is too "high-brow" for him. A mere glance through the magazine brings the conviction that the material is interesting, absorbing, and of benefit to everyone. A happy combination of the interesting and the literary have been attained with marked success.
>
> The first issue is an undeniable success, it now remains for the student-body to give its help and interest towards insuring future issues of a like high quality. The only thing remaining up to the editorial staff is to keep future publications up to the standards of the first issue.

But the *Schooner* was, at its inception, regarded as a campus phenomenon. Neither of the Lincoln dailies noticed its appearance, and the opening sale of subscriptions was almost entirely to students, faculty members, and campus organizations. Novices in the publishing field and modest in their anticipations, the staff of the *Schooner* made no attempt to startle the literary world with news of their entry into it. They mailed no announcements, they published no advertisements, and they offered no exchange copies to other journals already established in the field.

Instead they set about preparing a second issue to meet the announced deadline of April 1. This task was considerably simplified by the quality and success of the first issue. Having witnessed the magazine as a reality, many sought publication in it; by far the majority of the would-be contributors were again students, but faculty members and university staff employees showed increasing interest, and several manuscripts were received from outside the confines of the campus. The material selected for the ninety-page issue included four short stories, ten poems, six essays, and a verse drama. It also included what was to become a regular feature of the magazine, the "Ox Cart." That collection of editorial comments and information concerning contributors has since 1928 been written by Dr. Wimberly, but at this first appearance it was the work of Royce West.

The second issue presented the work of seven students, seven members of the university staff, and eight people not directly associated with the university. Noteworthy among the student contributions was the first magazine-published poem of Wilbur Gaffney, who today, after a long and varied career of writing and editing, is a professor of composition at the University of Nebraska. Faculty contributions included Wimberly's second published story, "Dispossessed"; a "spectacle" play by Professor Sherman, and an article on "Snake-Lore in the Central West" by Nebraska's most distinguished woman

scholar, Louise Pound. Most of the contributors from outside the university were graduates of it; among these was
Mildred Burcham, who was then teaching in Montana. Her
poem "Good-Bye" thus became the first contribution to make
the pages of the *Schooner* from outside the state of Nebraska.

The prefatory announcement in the second issue repeated
the wistfully tentative statement which accompanied the
Schooner's first appearance: "If there is sufficent interest in
the publication, the publishers will continue the issuance."
The very fact that a second issue appeared was, however, re-
assuring; it asserted the success of the first number, and it
demonstrated the existence of machinery necessary for continued publication.

The third issue, which appeared in July, sold almost 1,200
copies.[5] It began to appear that the magazine's future was
assured. And when Volume I, Number 4 appeared on November first, to mark the successful conclusion of the first year,
there was general rejoicing and optimism among members of
the *Schooner* staff. Robert Lasch, writing in the "Ox Cart"
for that issue, expressed the editorial sentiment (p. 303):

> The *Prairie Schooner* with this, the fourth number,
> is experiencing the delightful sensations of a young
> father. This issue marks the end of the first year of the
> *Prairie Schooner,* and its editors are indulging in con-
> gratulatory sentiments, directed not to themselves, but
> to a University public that has somehow been able to
> support a literary magazine for a whole year. This,
> after all, is the achievement extraordinary. The editors
> admit, modestly, that the struggle through four issues

[5] *Daily Nebraskan,* October 27, 1927, p. 1. This is a high circulation
for a little magazine. Hoffman points out (*op. cit.,* p. 2) that the circulation of such a magazine is generally under one thousand. The *Midland*
through most of its career had a circulation of about 500. And according
to Malcolm Cowley, Alfred Kreymbourg's fine poetry magazine *Others* had,
throughout its four years, a circulation of about 300 ("Magazine Business:
1910-46," *New Republic,* CXV, 521-522).

of the magazine's first year has been a ponderous one; but they are quite willing to hand all the laurels to the subscribers who have indicated once and for all that there is a place in Nebraska for such a publication as the *Schooner* aims to be.

The pride of achievement demonstrated in that statement was merited by the *Schooner*'s early success; and history has partially justified the optimistic note with which the remark concluded. Not even the most confident among the *Schooner* staff could have predicted the long and unbroken career which lay ahead. The *Schooner* was to continue through its second year and through its fifth. Despite the rigors of the depression years, it was to survive through a tenth volume, and despite World War II, through a twentieth. And with the Winter issue of 1951 the *Schooner* was to achieve the distinction of a quarter-century's uninterrupted publication. Of over four hundred American little magazines described in Hoffman's bibliography, only twelve, including the *Schooner,* have lived so long. Only three (*Voices, Parnassus,* and the *Prairie Schooner*) have survived twenty-five years under one title and one editor. And of those three, *Prairie Schooner* alone carries fiction.

3

Financial History

Despite the *Schooner*'s subsequent record of continuous publication, the optimism voiced by Robert Lasch in 1927 was in a way ill founded. For when the editors thanked the "subscribers who have indicated once and for all that there is a place in Nebraska for such a publication as the *Schooner* aims to be," they were still regarding the *Schooner* as a campus enterprise, to be supported primarily through sales to the university population. In retrospect it is evident that had the *Schooner* been forced to depend upon such support it would have collapsed within months of Lasch's optimistic editorial statement. Students whose natural curiosity had been fueled by the *Daily Nebraskan*'s publicity and who had therefore bought a copy or two of the early *Schooner* apparently decided that it was too "literary" for their tastes. It contained no jokes, cartoons, or colored pictures, and its stories seemed somewhat heavy for sophomoric diversion. The forty cents asked for a single copy of the *Schooner* would, at that time, buy eight copies of *Collier's, Liberty,* or the *Saturday Evening Post*. There were few, even among those students given to buying magazines, who valued the literary quality of the *Schooner* that highly.

So, instead of increasing as the founders had hoped, campus sales began to decline, and the *Schooner* had to seek financial help in order to survive. Just two issues after he had complimented the campus for its support, Lasch was forced to write (Spring, 1928, 147):

> This issue of the *Prairie Schooner,* together with the next three numbers, owes itself to a group of fine people in Lincoln who, when informed that the *Schooner* was financially disabled, turned in contributions enough to insure publication at least for the remainder of this year.
>
> The sincere gratitude of the editorial staff is assured those persons who contributed so generously.

The staff of the *Schooner* tried to muster campus enthusiasm. Each new issue was announced and extolled through a front-page story in the *Daily Nebraskan,* and feature stories frequently appeared between issues, to keep the *Schooner*'s name before the students. The price of the magazine was dropped, with the first issue of 1929, to thirty cents a copy or one dollar a year. And an annual subscription drive was inaugurated with special reduced prices to fraternities and sororities for block subscriptions of five or more. Wimberly made a show of confidence for public consumption; on October 12, 1928, he announced in the *Daily Nebraskan* that the most recent sales drive had "swelled the circulation of the Schooner immensely." But the increase was relative. By the end of 1929 Wimberly acknowledged the *Schooner*'s continued dependence on outside help (Fall, 1929, 303):

> With this issue the *Schooner* finishes its third year and announces itself ready to venture upon a fourth. Somehow or other we have managed to get along; so we propose to continue our journey undaunted by the bleaching bones—the bones of this or that magazine— which line the pioneer trails. There have been desert days when we feared that we could not stumble or crawl

from one water-hole to the next. But the water-holes
are there if only one has the hardihood and faith to
carry on. Nor has manna been wanting. We have our
good angels, all of whom we should like to mention
here by name. But good angels do not care for public
acknowledgment; hence we refrain.

The most important of these good angels was the university
itself, which, through the office of Chancellor E. A. Burnett,
provided not a regular appropriation but emergency subsidies
totaling approximately $200 annually through 1929 and 1930.
But even such emergency aid could not have supported the
Schooner had its sales been restricted to the campus. The
Schooner's salvation resulted primarily from the fact that
shortly after its founding the magazine had begun to draw subscriptions from outside the city of Lincoln. Libraries and colleges throughout Nebraska were among the first subscribers
to extend the *Schooner*'s sphere. And the neighboring city of
Omaha provided a market for many copies of the *Schooner,*
both through newsstand sale and through subscriptions. In
1929 Mrs. Myrtle Mason, working through the Omaha
Woman's Press Club, sold some seventy subscriptions in that
city.

The most surprising and encouraging boost to the tottering
Schooner, however, came from outside the state. Although its
editors made no attempt to advertise the *Schooner* nationally,
the magazine was soon known far beyond the borders of Nebraska. By the time it was three years old, it was receiving
correspondence from such distant places as New Mexico and
North Carolina, California and New York, Canada and
Switzerland.

How did such widespread recognition come about? It was
in part attributable to the early contributors who, leaving the
university, carried the *Prairie Schooner* with them. Thus
Helene Magaret, a contributor to the first volume of the
Schooner, wrote to Wimberly in November, 1929:

When I first came to New York I called on Mr. Lee Foster Hartman of "Harper's Magazine." At that time he told me that they were particularly interested in new short story writers and were looking to the small middle-western magazines for their material, and asked me to suggest any magazine I might be acquainted with. Of course, I recommended "The Prairie Schooner."[1]

In July of the same year Margaret Christie, New York literary agent, wrote to Marie Macumber: "I lent your short stories in the *Prairie Schooner* to one of the editors of the John Day Company who returned them a few minutes ago saying, 'That woman, Marie Macumber, is well worth watching—has she done a novel? What an excellent book The Prairie Schooner is.'" And the following month, August, 1929, Miss Christie wrote again to Miss Macumber: "Do tell Mr. Wimberly that at least one half dozen editors have seen the *Prairie Schooner* on my desk and looked it over with pleasure."

It is impossible to estimate how much missionary work was carried on by *Schooner* contributors without being thus recorded. But certainly many of the founders and early contributors remained in close contact with the writing and publishing field, and one can imagine that their influence in the *Schooner*'s behalf was considerable.

Another agent which served to advertise the *Schooner*'s name was the *Writer's Digest* index of markets. Beginning in 1928 it carried the name and a brief description of the *Schooner* in its listings. But more immediate, and probably more important, in spreading the reputation of the early *Schooner* was recognition by the two leading short-story anthologies of the day, the Edward J. O'Brien annual *Best Short Stories* and the *O. Henry Memorial Award* series.

The O'Brien anthology, which had been published annually since 1915, carried as a regular appendix a "Yearbook

[1] Unpublished letters quoted or referred to in this study are, unless otherwise noted, in the possession of Dr. Wimberly.

of the American Short Story." In that appendix, stories regarded as "distinctive" in quality were honored with one, two,
or three asterisks, depending on their relative merit, and magazines were rated according to the number and percentage of
distinctive stories they had published during the year. The
first O'Brien volume in which the *Schooner* was considered
was that for 1928, covering the period of August, 1927, through
June, 1928.

O'Brien's reaction to the young *Schooner* was probably the
biggest boost the magazine ever received. He had considered
well over a hundred magazines in making his selections for the
year. Of those, ninety-six, including fourteen little magazines, had published distinctive stories. Listed as having published fifty per cent or more of distinctive stories were thirteen
magazines, including four little magazines: *Dial, Midland,
Transition,* and *Prairie Schooner.* Of these thirteen, four
were given a perfect rating of one hundred per cent, indicating that every story published by those magazines during
the year had been distinctive. Those four were the quality
magazines *Harper's* and *Bookman* and the little magazines
Dial and *Prairie Schooner.*

In a letter dated May 21, 1929 (reprinted Spring, 1929,
235-236), O'Brien wrote to Wimberly:

> The quality of its stories, articles, and poems is such
> that the *Prairie Schooner* ranks with the *Midland,* the
> *Frontier* and not more than one or two other Ameri-
> can periodicals, as the most significant expression of
> American life which we possess. As such, it focuses the
> whole cultural life of a section of America. As an ex-
> perienced reader of American stories, I find it more vital
> as an interpretation of American life than the *Atlantic
> Monthly,* the *Forum,* or *Harper's* magazine. I know
> that New York editors watch it carefully and English
> men of letters to whose attention I have called it find
> that is gives them a clearer picture of American life in
> its creative aspects than most American periodicals.

On the day of that tribute by O'Brien, Blanche Colton Williams, then editor of the *O. Henry Memorial* anthology, wrote asking that she be placed on the *Schooner* mailing list. In the appendix to the anthology for 1929, the *Prairie Schooner* was listed (between *Popular* and *Romance*) as one of the eighty magazines considered for the selections and short-story ratings. The list was composed primarily of popular magazines, pulps and slicks, and included only one other little magazine, the *Frontier*. The *Schooner*'s inclusion on that list was not, like the O'Brien rating, any sign of special merit, but it did serve to place the *Schooner*'s name before people who otherwise might not have heard of it.

During the years 1928 and 1929 the *Schooner*'s poetry also brought the magazine recognition. The *Literary Digest* for March 10, 1928, reprinted Amy Bruner Almy's poem "Where the Mesquite Grows" (Winter, 1928). And Helene Magaret's poem "Legs" (Winter, 1929) was selected by William S. Braithwaite for inclusion in his *Anthology of Magazine Verse for 1929*. Both reprints served to advertise the *Schooner*'s name. And the inclusion of Miss Magaret's poem in Braithwaite's anthology was a distinct achievement for the magazine, for that anthology was to America's poetry about what O'-Brien's annual was to its fiction.

Even as campus interest was dwindling, then, the *Schooner* was beginning to acquire a larger reputation. It was not, by any means, a popular reputation; recognition came almost exclusively from those relative few who, whether as writers, editors, or simply readers, interest themselves closely in the course of current literature. But it was a sound reputation. And it began to produce results in the *Schooner* office. Most of the mail which came from outside the state brought manuscripts or inquiries regarding submissions, but a gratifying number of letters brought money to inaugurate subscriptions.

With the aid of these new subscribers from other states and with modest financial aid from the university, the *Schooner* continued through 1930. In the "Ox Cart" for Fall, 1930, Wimberly announced: "With this issue the *Schooner* is four years of age, a fact in which it takes a kind of Methuselah pride. Such longevity is not, you know, commonly the fate of the smaller magazine."

But things were happening outside the *Schooner* office—things that constituted a new and unforeseen threat to the magazine's existence. The depression had begun, in the East, and reverberations were already being felt in the Midlands.

The most immediate danger to the *Schooner* was the threatened withdrawal of university support. Anticipating a financial crisis, Chancellor Burnett and the Board of Regents of the University were by 1931 seeking places where the annual budget might be reduced, and support for the *Schooner* seemed a likely item for elimination. That support had originally been given in the belief that the magazine was primarily a campus enterprise. The number of student subscriptions had dipped to an alarming low—about two hundred in 1931.[2] Furthermore, university students, and even Nebraskans as a whole, were by this time in the minority among the contributors to the magazine. Wimberly was informed by Chancellor Burnett that because the *Schooner* could not properly be called a university activity, it could not expect continued financial support.

Wimberly frankly admits today that, small though the university subsidy was in 1931, its removal would have meant the end of the *Prairie Schooner*. And he gives full credit for the *Schooner's* continued publication to unexpected support from an influential friend, the Omaha *World-Herald*. The *Herald* was in the 1930's, as it is today, the most widely read and the most politically powerful newspaper in Nebraska. It had, in 1931, a total Sunday circulation of over 114,000 copies, more than half of which were distributed outside the city of Omaha.

[2] Compare the popularity of the campus humor magazine, *Awgwan*, which according to the *Daily Nebraskan* for February 12, 1931, sold 1,900 copies in that month.

This powerful organ had been friendly toward the *Schooner* from the start, frequently devoting news space to the coverage of a new *Schooner* issue. And on Sunday, September 27, 1931, having heard that essential support to the *Schooner* might be withdrawn, the paper devoted the leading editorial to a 900-word consideration of the *Schooner*'s plight. George Grimes, who wrote the editorial, praised the magazine and pointed out its value to the university and to the state. He accused the students, the faculty, and the regents of failing to appreciate that value, and then made his appeal—or more properly, his threat—in tones which could not be misunderstood:

> The plight of the Schooner, the indifference of students and faculty, the economy of the regents, raise, very seriously, the question as to what the university is doing, and whether it is justifying the confidence of the people of the state and the taxes that are spent in its support. . . .
>
> The people of Nebraska have just ground for sternly challenging the university for its failure to support its distinctive magazine. . . . The people of Nebraska have a right to scrutinize the accounts of a board of regents which is fearful of appropriating $250 a year for such a magazine. . . .
>
> The Prairie Schooner's hard row suggests that the university regents, chancellor and faculty should take stern stock of themselves and their work. If they care so little for this one distinctive thing, it is fair to assume that they care little for many. If they fail so miserably to get across their message to the students in this one aspect of cultural life, it is fair to assume that they fail also in other messages.

It is ordinarily difficult to estimate the influence exerted by a single newspaper editorial; but the practical effect of this blast from the *World-Herald* cannot be questioned. Wimberly recalls that the day after the editorial appeared he was summoned to the office of Chancellor Burnett, where he denied charges that he had incited the attack on the university administration. He told the chancellor that he had not been aware of the impending attack until Grimes called him to verify a point of information, and that he had no knowledge as to the source of Grimes's original tip.

But regardless of Wimberly's role in initiating or encouraging the *World-Herald*'s editorial, he has never (apart perhaps from a few uncomfortable moments in the chancellor's office) had reason to regret its appearance. The university subsidy, which he had been resigned to losing, was continued, and with its aid the *Schooner* remained in business. Wimberly's relief prompted a show of confidence in the "Ox Cart" for the first (Winter) issue of 1932:

> In its title the *Prairie Schooner* carries a reminiscence of hard but brave times, of those days when it took undying faith and courage to whip the oxen along in the general direction of the next settlement or the next water hole. Hence, the *Schooner* does not, the chances are, feel a small matter like the Depression as keenly as do certain other magazines. . . .
>
> For still another, and perhaps a better, reason the *Schooner* will be comparatively unaffected by the current Depression or, for that matter, by any depression whatsoever. . . . It has never had any money to lose. Consequently, it can't be depressed by a loss of what it has never had. Financially, it is just as flourishing as it ever was. It was hard up when it started out six years ago. It has been hard up ever since. And it hasn't any hopes of being less hard up six years from now.

There is, of course, a note of shrillness in the facetious bravado of those remarks. Wimberly was, as he well realized at the time, whistling in the teeth of a growing gale. America's little magazines were beginning to fall before that gale at a rapid and generally increasing rate: eight in 1930, thirteen in 1931, sixteen in 1932, nine in 1933, thirty-nine (including Frederick's *Midland*) in 1934, thirty-two in 1935. These magazines were failing for the lack of subscribers and, hence, of

adequate income. And there was an imminent danger of the
Schooner's failing for the same reason. Although the *World-
Herald* editorial had been successful in its effect on the chancellor and the board of regents, it had been less successful in
its appeal to the students and faculty. Campus subscriptions
remained pathetically few. Furthermore, through 1932 and
the years that followed, more and more of those letters from
outside the state which had formerly brought money for subscriptions brought, instead, appeals like the following:

> Please tell Mr. Williams [the business manager] not
> to remove my name from the subscription list. I'll send
> in my dollar as soon as I get it. (December, 1932)

> I am enclosing twenty-five cents postage. For this
> I would like to have you send me the last four copies
> of the Prairie Schooner. (February, 1934)

> I am enclosing three cents in stamps, which I trust
> will defray the expenditure of sending me a sample
> copy. If my present job (secretary to the relief officer of
> this county) holds out, I hope to subscribe to your pub-
> lication. (March, 1935)

By the beginning of 1933 loss of sales was approaching
fatal proportions. To reduce expenses, the size of the magazine was cut drastically. Whereas the four issues of 1932 (Volume 6) had averaged eighty-six pages, the Spring and Summer
issues of 1933 each contained only thirty pages, and the Fall
issue of that year thirty-four. To save money on postage, Wimberly began driving to Omaha and personally delivering magazines to the newsstands there. Even with such savings, the cut
in expenses did not keep pace with the loss of income. The
Schooner was tottering. Rumors of its impending demise
(many of them started by Wimberly's remarks in letters of
rejection) circulated widely, and the *Windsor Quarterly*
actually carried, in its issue for Summer, 1933, a report of the
Schooner's discontinuance. Letters of sympathy and encourage-

ment poured into the *Schooner* office from previous contributors and from editors of other magazines. But those who
so generously offered moral support were themselves in no
condition to offer anything more tangible.

In the midst of these difficulties, as the *Schooner* staff was
striving to stretch its few dollars from one issue to the next,
came another threat of the withdrawal of university support.
Because of declining enrollment, reduced appropriations from
taxation money, and reduction in federal funds, the university
was in serious financial difficulty. The budget for the fiscal
year beginning July 1, 1933, had to show a reduction of more
than twenty per cent from that for the previous year. To
help effect that saving, all salaries of $1,500 and over were
reduced twenty-two per cent, and salaries below that figure
were cut to the cost of refilling the positions with new appli-
cants. Other means of achieving the cut included elimination
of the School of Fine Arts and consolidation of its structure as
a department in the College of Arts and Sciences; elimination
of seventy-two staff positions in addition to not filling positions
left vacant by deaths; elimination of all tuition scholarships
and reduction of graduate scholarships and assistantships by
about twenty-five per cent; considerable curtailment of work
at off-campus agricultural stations; and the closing of two wards
in the University Hospital in Omaha.[3]

In view of such drastic economies, elimination of support
to the *Schooner* would appear to have been almost inevitable.
But once more an influential friend saved the magazine. This
time it was C. H. Oldfather, Dean of the College of Arts and
Sciences, who had replaced John D. Hicks in that position only
the year before. Oldfather knew the value to the university of
the *Schooner*'s prestige and was anxious that the magazine be
continued. He first appealed to the deans' committee, in
April, 1933, and secured that body's unanimous support for

[3] *Daily Nebraskan*, September 10, 1933, pp. 1, 4.

continuing the subsidy. He then approached the chancellor and suggested that it would be dangerous to allow the *Schooner* to die. His letter to Wimberly, dated April 28, 1933, describes the interview:

> The Chancellor was speaking of where criticism would focus in case of certain cuts and eliminations in the University. There was the idea among some people that criticism aroused by drastic cuts would focus upon the legislature. I said that this was possible but it was also just as possible that it would focus upon the administration. Then I went on: For instance, should we eliminate the subsidy for the *Prairie Schooner,* where would the criticism which would arise from the World Herald and the [Lincoln] Star focus? Would it not focus on the administration which could not divert $250 used to whitewash the dressing room in the Stadium to the maintenance of so important a literary periodical? I think he got the point.

That particular point had, of course, been considerably sharpened by the *World-Herald* editorial of two years before; and apparently Chancellor Burnett did get it. At any rate, despite the severity of other budgetary reductions, aid to the *Schooner* was continued.

About a month after Oldfather's appeal to the administration, an attempt was made to capture the entire student body as subscribers to the *Schooner* and thus provide a source of assured income which would have ended the magazine's financial worries. A student activity tax plan was proposed, under which all students would pay a fixed annual fee covering athletic tickets, convocation fees, student council fees, contributions to the student union building fund, and subscriptions to four campus publications: the *Daily Nebraskan,* the *Cornhusker* yearbook, the *Awgwan* humor magazine, and the *Prairie Schooner*. In one of the largest referendums in the history of the university, the students voted two to one in favor of the general tax plan. But they voted against including four of the suggested items under the plan: the student council fee, the convocation fee, the building fund assessment, and the subscription to the *Schooner*.[4]

Despite this campus rebuff, the *Schooner* continued to appear. The *Daily Nebraskan* for September 10, 1933, announced the fact:

> Definite assurance that the Prairie Schooner will appear again on the campus this winter was released yesterday by Harry Foster, business manager of the publication.
>
> Considerable doubt had been manifested as to whether or not the Prairie Schooner would continue to function because of low funds, but it is now known that it will do so.

It was now obvious, however, that there was no quick and easy road to financial security, and that the continuation of the *Schooner* depended on an ability to sell it to people not cheerfully disposed to buy.

The years that followed witnessed a series of sales drives so close together as to be almost continuous. Through all those drives the *Schooner* staff had the close cooperation of the *Daily Nebraskan,* which frequently devoted front-page space to the promotional plans and their results.

On March 6, 1934, the *Nebraskan* announced, with a flourish, the first of the several subscription drives:

> In an effort to acquaint the people of the Middle West with its character, the Prairie Schooner is launching on Thursday, March 8, a campaign of expansion. This program will be somewhat in the nature of a debut for the Prairie Schooner on the campus.

That drive, conducted by fifty students under the leadership of Gwen Thompson and Roberta Lohrmann, featured twenty dollars in cash prizes to those obtaining the most subscriptions

[4] *Daily Nebraskan*, September 10, 1933, p. 1.

on campus. The goal of the campaign was five hundred new subscriptions; it obtained a total of 277.

In the fall of 1934 Herbert Behlen, the new business manager, went to work on newsstand circulation, placing the *Schooner* on fourteen stands in Lincoln and several in surrounding towns. And in December, Behlen inaugurated an elaborate drive which included radio advertising, a reduced price of twenty-five cents a copy to students, a door-to-door campaign conducted by the women's advertising sorority Gamma Alpha Chi, and a slogan contest with a $7.50 cash award. Two hundred facscimiles of the *Schooner* cover bearing the winning slogan "Pulse of the Prairie People" were distributed on the campus.

In February of 1935 Behlen undertook a campaign through the mails, sending two groups of form letters. The first group, numbering 650, went to university libraries throughout the country, Nebraska public libraries not already subscribing, and university faculty members. The second group, numbering 3,500, was planned and mailed in cooperation with the Alumni Association; it offered Nebraska alumni living in Lincoln a special combination rate on subscriptions to the *Schooner* and the *Nebraska Alumnus* magazine.

While Behlen was working to increase the off-campus circulation, the members of Gamma Alpha Chi were again conducting a campaign to build sales and subscriptions among the students. With the aid of the *Daily Nebraskan*, they tried to convince the students that the *Schooner* was not so "literary" as to be uninteresting. Pointing specifically to one humorous story (Dwight Perkins' "A. W. Vodding vs. The Claus Co."), the press copy described the Winter issue as "going popular," "catering to the student taste," "limiting its classical fiction," "emphasizing popular magazine material"—"a campus appeal edition."

Applied to the *Schooner*, such phrases were more deceptive than descriptive. The magazine had undergone no major change in policy; it was not, in tone or content, truly "popular," and it was certainly far from being collegiate. The advertising device employed in behalf of the *Schooner* can be justified only on the premise that the end justifies the means. The end in this case was, ultimately, to preserve a good little magazine—immediately, to sell copies of the *Schooner* to Nebraska students. And the means was effective enough to be continued; the "popular appeal" device remained a part of the *Schooner*'s publicity program through several succeeding issues.

But a somewhat misleading sales appeal was not the most spectacular promotional device ever employed by the *Schooner*, nor was it the most questionable. Among the devices of the next few years, which included more circular letters, prize contests, drives by the Y.W.C.A., display booths on the campus, special rates for block subscriptions, and a more attractive cover, two devices are outstanding.

Probably the most spectacular was the use of one entire issue of the *Daily Nebraskan* for publicizing the *Schooner*. The *Nebraskan* for Tuesday, November 9, 1937, carried no news items or regular features. It contained two editorials extolling the virtues of the *Schooner* and urging students to subscribe; the rest of its space was devoted to reprints of material from the current *Schooner* (Fall, 1937), which had gone on sale only the day before. The *Nebraskan* reprinted very nearly the whole of that *Schooner*, carrying four of the five stories and fourteen of the seventeen poems, in addition to an excerpt from the "Ox Cart." The bold device took the campus completely by surprise and doubtless caused more comment than any combination of earlier publicity techniques. A front-page story in the *Nebraskan* for the following day describes the commotion which the novel issue had created on the campus and the pandemonium in the printing office, where press runs had been delayed while printers and proofreaders read, with mixed reactions, the unusual copy.

The most devious attempt at building sales was reported in the *Daily Nebraskan* on November 1, 1940:

> Student manuscripts may be printed in the Prairie Schooner, university literary quarterly, under a new editorial policy announced by Dr. L. C. Wimberly, editor. Formerly, only works of nationally established authors have been admitted for publication.
>
> Short stories, articles, one-act plays, poems, biographies, and other student writing may be submitted provided the manuscript has been approved by the author's English instructor. All entries should maintain the usual standard of the Prairie Schooner, according to Wimberly. Therefore, students submitting manuscripts will be required to subscribe to the magazine for a year that they might study the type of literature wanted.
>
> "We feel that this experience of writing for a specific publication and the likelihood of the reward for good work being the appearance in print of students' offerings alongside those of authors of established reputation should prove a great stimulus to student literary work," said Dr. Wimberly.

Apart from the unrealistic pretense that a year's subscription to the *Schooner* would have some magical salutary effect on a manuscript submitted at the time of the writer's subscribing, that statement of policy contains a patent misrepresentation. Students had been submitting manuscripts to the magazine, with or without the approval of their English instructors, since before the first issue appeared, to the advantage of the *Schooner* as well as of the students. Some of the most important names in the *Schooner*'s list of early "discoveries" are those of people who first contributed as students.[5]

But the questionable ethics of that attempt to inveigle subscriptions are perhaps not so significant in a study of the

[5] See pp. 125-128.

Schooner as the situation which permitted such an attempt. The *Prairie Schooner*'s publicity over the preceding years not only had admitted the use of student manuscripts but had consciously advertised the fact, as an inducement for students to subscribe. The point had been made scores of times in the pages of the *Nebraskan*. The assumption that the student body could be deceived into believing that acceptance of student submissions constituted a "new editorial policy" was thus a tacit admission that the *Schooner*'s publicity attempts had been ineffective.

In general, such seems to have been the case. At any rate, the various sales drives had failed to make the *Schooner* popular on the campus. On December 3, 1935, shortly *after* H. P. Behlen's extensive letter campaign and Gamma Alpha Chi's canvass of the campus, the new business manager, Frank Smith, reported in the *Nebraskan*: "Of the six hundred issues of the fall Prairie Schooner distributed, about 25 per cent of that number went to student subscribers." In the fall of 1931 the student subscriptions had totaled about two hundred. Now, after four years of strenuous campaigning for campus circulation, that number had dropped to about 150. By the summer of 1937, despite intervening drives for subscriptions, circulation had fallen off until suspension of the magazine seemed imminent; Wimberly hinted in the "Ox Cart" (pp. 194, 196) that the Summer issue might be the magazine's last. Five years and many campaigns later, on November 17, 1942, the *Nebraskan* carried another reference to the lack of student subscriptions: "Rated as one of the ten best magazines of its kind in the nation, the Schooner, due to lack of support of its home state, and particularly of the university where it was founded and is printed, will be forced to go off campus unless the subscription list increases substantially."

It must not be assumed, however, that the many drives for subscriptions had been entirely fruitless. Viewing their object as the preservation of the *Schooner,* they had been clearly successful. For although they had not succeeded in building a large circulation, they had retarded the loss of circulation. It was not unusual for a single drive to bring in 100 or 150 new subscriptions. Without such boosts, the circulation of the *Schooner* would have declined, by the early 1930's, to a point below which it would hardly have justified publication of the magazine. The extreme importance of those drives for subscriptions, and of the various student business managers who directed them, is pointed up by the fact that after H. P. Behlen resigned in 1936 Wimberly announced that the *Schooner* would be forced to suspend publication unless a new business manager could be found immediately. (With the appointment of Lyle Fitch a few days later, the *Schooner* continued.)

In retrospect, it is remarkable that the *Schooner* survived its first dozen years. The history of those years is a series of crises, any one of which could easily have marked the termination of the magazine's career. The thing primarily responsible for preserving the *Schooner* was Wimberly's strong desire to keep it alive. With the aid of a constantly changing staff, a few influential friends, and a benevolent fate, he accomplished that desire. But the existence of the *Schooner* was so tenuous as to be unnerving. Frequently Wimberly did not know two weeks before the appointed date for publication whether the next issue of the *Schooner* would appear or not. Not only did financial worries take time from his job as editor, but the uncertainty surrounding the *Schooner*'s publication complicated his job of accepting manuscripts for publication. As he grew older, the burden of continuing the *Schooner* weighed more heavily on him. It is a moot question how long he might have carried the burden had there been no change in the *Schooner*'s organization. What the magazine clearly needed was a strong permanent sponsor.

Gradually, over a period of several years, the *Schooner* acquired such a sponsor—the University of Nebraska. Ostensibly the change in the *Schooner*'s status came with the Summer issue of 1937. Previously, the statement of publication had indicated that the *Schooner* was "sponsored by the Wordsmith Chapter of Sigma Upsilon" and published "with the aid of the University of Nebraska." But with this issue the statement was changed to read: "It is sponsored by, and published with the aid of, the University of Nebraska." Actually that change in statement was simply a recognition of the situation which had for some years existed. The fraternity responsible for founding the *Schooner* had long ceased to take any active part in its administration; from the first issue the *Schooner's* chief sponsor, financially, had been the university. But the statement did imply a greater responsibility on the part of the university, and in the years that followed, the university assumed that responsibility.

Beginning in 1937, the magazine was copyrighted in the name of the university, and with the first issue of 1939 the front cover carried for the first time the information "Published at the University of Nebraska." In 1940 a permanent fund was established for university studies, to include the *Prairie Schooner,* and the cover was changed to read "Published by the University of Nebraska." In October of 1941 Emily Schossberger was made executive secretary of the University Board of Publications, which among other duties administered the *Schooner* funds, and with the next issue she became an honorary editor of the magazine. Beginning with the first issue of 1943 the *Schooner* was copyrighted by the newly instituted University of Nebraska Press, of which Miss Schossberger was editor. Shortly thereafter the duties of the business manager were transferred to the office of the Press, and Joanna Radke, last of the student managers, was succeeded by Margaret Seely, the first of several paid employees who have since conducted the *Schooner's* business affairs. Finally, with the first issue of 1947, the magazine appeared "Sponsored by the University of Nebraska Press," and Miss Schossberger was listed as an advisory editor.

Several financial windfalls have come to the *Schooner* during and since the university's gradual adoption of the magazine. For example, five of its articles have been reprinted by the *Reader's Digest*, bringing the *Schooner* in one case as much as $600. And with the volume for 1951 the *Schooner* began to sell advertising space to binderies and publishers, for which space it received as much as $80 an issue.[6] But the sponsorship by the university has not worked financial miracles for the magazine. Circulation has remained pathetically small. When Volume 25, Number 4 appeared in 1951, to conclude the quarterly's twenty-fifth year, the *Schooner* had a subscription list of 438, only 380 of which were paid subscriptions.[7] Maintenance of that circulation has continued to depend largely upon campus drives for subscriptions, and these drives are still conducted by various student organizations. (Outstanding among such drives was that planned and directed by Kurt Porjes, student business manager, in the spring of 1943, which brought in more than two hundred new subscriptions.)

University sponsorship has not, then, made the *Schooner* a profitable venture. Nevertheless, it has considerably improved the *Schooner*'s general stability.

---

[6] The advertising rate is $40 a page (inside front, inside back, or outside back cover). The *Schooner* had, of course, carried advertising before. The first three volumes contained advertising from Lincoln bookstores at $12.50 a page, and since 1940 the *Schooner* had carried exchange advertisements from a number of other magazines and publishing houses.

[7] The total circulation of the issue was distributed as follows:

Complimentary copies (publishing houses, chancellor and regents, editorial board, etc.)	30
Exchanges with other magazines	28
Total free	58
Library subscriptions (in thirty states, the District of Columbia, sixteen foreign countries or territories)	71
Faculty subscriptions	29
Student subscriptions	11
Other paid subscriptions	269
Total paid	380
Total circulation	438

One obvious advantage resulting from the university's control is a more liberal operating budget. Deficit appropriations for the *Schooner* have, since 1940, far exceeded the aid which Wimberly was able to procure before that time. During the fiscal year beginning July 1, 1945, for example, the magazine cost the university $364. The annual costs for the next four years were $802, $727, $873, and $227. And during the year beginning July 1, 1950, the expense to the university was $1,141, or more than thirty-five cents for every copy of the *Schooner* printed during that year. Despite the fact that the price of the *Schooner* had doubled since 1942,[8] income from sales and subscriptions during the same period was $1,112, slightly less than that from university appropriations.

It should not be assumed from the size of those expenditures that had the *Schooner* continued to function under its earlier independent organization it would have required subsidization to that extent. Since it has been supported through the Publications Fund, the *Schooner* has been charged for items never before among its expenses. Among the disbursements, for example, have been annual charges for "salaries and assistance" ranging from about $125 to $210. That money has all gone to pay for services (exclusive of the cost of printing) rendered in the University Press office; before the University's adoption of the magazine nobody ever received a penny in wages for his work on the *Schooner* staff. Wimberly has never been compensated. Again, the large total expenditure for the year 1950-1951 included $537.85 for "properties and improvements." That is more than was spent on the *Schooner*'s physical properties during its first fifteen years under independent organization. Beginning with the Spring issue of 1947 the *Schooner*

[8] In 1942 the *Schooner* still sold for 30c a copy, $1.00 a year. The price was raised twice in 1943: first to 35c a copy, then to 45c a copy, $1.50 a year. In 1948 it was again raised, to 60c a copy, $2.00 a year, at which level it has continued. Faculty members, however, are offered a special price of $1.50 a year.

appeared in a new and attractive cover. It had undergone several changes in cover design before, nine times not counting minor changes in print or color. But never had the *Schooner* had a cover like this one, which was designed by Miriam Woods at a cost of $100.

This greater liberality with *Schooner* funds under university sponsorship has, of course, operated to the advantage of the magazine. The *Schooner* is physically more attractive in its handsome new cover and its consistent size than it was during the dark days of the middle 1930's. And its business affairs are more efficiently handled in the competently staffed, well equipped Press office than they were at a time when half of the business office was Dr. Wimberly's file cabinet and the other half the middle drawer in some student's desk.

But one of the biggest advantages accruing to the *Schooner* from its new mode of operation is not one of external appearance or business efficiency. It is something considerably more important. Wimberly has been freed from the technical and financial worries attending the *Schooner*'s publication. This has enabled him to spend more time criticizing, selecting, and working over the material which is to make up the *Schooner*'s contents. Furthermore, with the university's backing he has a reasonable assurance that the magazine he starts to plan in July will appear in October and that it will be of the size he anticipates. In the history of the *Schooner*, Wimberly has served as delivery boy and copy boy, proofreader and secretary, salesman, public relations man, and business manager. Today all the time he spends on the *Schooner* can be devoted to the proper duties of the position which he has always held—that of editor.

4

Editorial Policy: Regionalism

T HE drama of a little magazine may lie in the story of its struggle to survive, but the identifying characteristic of any magazine, the key to a real understanding of what the magazine *is,* lies in its editorial policy. The contents of a magazine differ with each new issue, yet we recognize a continuing identity. A complete alteration of format or even a change of title may superficially disguise the identity of a magazine but cannot destroy it any more than loss of weight, plastic surgery, and a new name could destroy the real identity of a friend. Editorial policy, which is to the magazine what character is to the man, permits us to recognize a continuity of existence and identity which other aspects of a magazine could not establish. This is not to say that editorial policies ever are, or ideally should be, static. A magazine which is to maintain any vitality must be prepared to grow and develop, to adjust to new situations. But any real revolution in editorial policy creates, in effect, a new magazine.

A magazine's editorial policy is, like a man's character, more easily felt or observed than defined. It is a complex of many factors: broad purposes and self-appointed functions, social and political attitudes, critical judgments. It is exhibited in the type, themes, style, tone, quality, and length of the selections which the magazine prints. It may be shaped or influenced by such widely divergent forces as the place and circumstances of the magazine's publication, the personal tastes and prejudices of its editor or editors, the interests of its chief supporters, the availability of manuscripts, and the pressure of changes in the national social or literary atmosphere.

As a first step toward defining a magazine's policy, one customarily identifies the school or movement to which the magazine belongs. Many—perhaps most—of America's little magazines have not adopted an editorial policy in this broad sense, but rather have been born of one. They have been established as purveyors, by enunciation or illustration, of specific doctrines or parties, advocates of political or critical movements. Thus the *Masses* and *Left Front* were created as left wing organs, *View* and *VVV* to voice surrealism, *Furioso* to further the new and experimental poetry, and the *Journal of American Poetry* to sustain the old and traditional.

The *Prairie Schooner*, in contrast, was created as an outlet not for artists of a particular political or critical bent but for those living in a specific geographical region. Its self-appointed task, at its inception, was to provide "an outlet for literary work in the University of Nebraska and a medium for the publication of the finest writing of the prairie country." Although not a declaration of critical bias, that statement does imply an editorial restriction, the nature of which is suggested by an article appearing in the first issue of the *Schooner*. There Bess Streeter Aldrich, writing at Wimberly's invitation, pointed out that ". . . a story rings most true when it is drawn from material within the limitations of our geographical, mental, or emotional boundaries." She continued (p. 81):

> Under the assumption that the new magazine will find its readers at present among the University students and specifically among those interested in writing, this mes-

sage is, frankly and without apology, a plea to those coming writers to make use of their native material. I believe there should come from Nebraska a select group of young writers to tell simply and clearly the story of the land that is neither east nor west.

Wimberly, who charted the *Schooner's* course from its beginning, is himself a strong advocate of this doctrine that literary creation can demonstrate conviction and authenticity only if it emerges from the artist's own experience:

> Which means that all literary writing is autobiographical—a transcript of the writer's unique moods, his unique auditory and optical sensations or illusions, his peculiar aches and pains, hopes, despairs, cynicisms, innate devilishness, and congenital tendency to laugh or weep. It means that the writer, if a native of Wahoo, Nebraska, must comport himself in the exercise of the literary art, as a Wahooan—as, say, a third-generation Swedish-American. Make what contortions he will he arrives at literary expression in the character of a Scandinavian-American, born and bred in Wahoo. He may envy the literary achievements of an eighth-generation Irish-American of Boston, and he may attempt to imitate the writing of the Irishman, but even his imitation will be Wahooesque.
> A citizen of Wahoo, then, or of Peoria, Illinois—if his experience, especially his early experience, has been confined to one or the other of those places—should stick to Wahoo or Peoria when he attempts to create character, background, situation.[1]

---

[1] Fall, 1946, 230. *Cf.* Frederick's editorial in the *Midland,* XVI, 153 (May-June, 1928) : "Let us recognize the increasingly definite dichotomous division of American life, and accept its significance for literature. The man or woman whose thirty or forty years have been lived in a universe of paved streets and apartments must not expect to write adequately of country life on the strength of a month's vacation at a summer resort. The writer born and bred in the small town, or on a farm, must recognize his inability to render easily and promptly the essential spirit of the metropolis. Sound fiction can proceed only from sustained and intimate experience."

Thus in restricting geographically the region from which the *Schooner* was to draw, the editors indicated a regional editorial policy. In establishing an outlet for midwestern writers they established an outlet for midwestern themes and ideas, characters and settings. That regional policy was further defined through editorial comments in the first few volumes of the *Schooner*. In the magazine's second year Wimberly repeated, in the "Ox Cart," the avowal that "our purpose is to give publication to the best literary writing we can find here in Lincoln and anywhere in the Midwest" (Summer, 1928, 233), and two issues later he spoke of the magazine as having its feet "pretty firmly planted on the soil of the Midwest" (Winter, 1929, 76). In the following issue a more active regionalism was indicated in associate editor R. T. Prescott's announcement (p. 173): "The *Schooner* editors are interested in finding a body of common feelings and traditions for midwesterners."

The early *Schooner* was thus a magazine devoted not only to the works of midwestern writers but to the portrayal of the region and the expression of its culture. It had assumed, as its editorial foundation, a policy of midwestern regionalism.

Regionalism as a literary movement is not easily characterized. The definition of the term varies with the subject to which it is applied. It has been used to include the local color of Bret Harte and the objective description of John Muir, the sentimental humor of James Whitcomb Riley and the terse grimness of Mary Wilkins Freeman. The term denotes simply that geographical restriction of subject matter discussed above; its connotations, however, are many and varied, and it is these connotations which are significant. Rather than attempt to examine the *Prairie Schooner* in terms of regionalism, then, one could perhaps more profitably examine midwestern regionalism in terms of the *Prairie Schooner*. Midwestern regionalism, that is, as it appeared in the late 1920's.

As exhibited in the early *Prairie Schooner,* midwestern regionalism displays, as concomitants of geographical restriction, a factual realism, a historical preoccupation, an emphasis on natural environment, a starkness often pessimistic, and a pride often defensive. These various elements all stem from the geographical emphasis, and are closely interrelated.

Taking a geographical section as his subject matter and the delineation of that section as his task, the twentieth-century regionalist quite naturally adopts an approach which is realistic. Only by close attention to essential detail can he make his definition authentic; and inauthenticity not only represents a failure of purpose but also alienates the regionalist's most devoted audience—those who know what the region is and reject any misrepresentation of it.

An editorial declaration of the *Schooner*'s devotion to this factual realism appears in the "Ox Cart" for the Winter, 1929 issue. There Martin S. Peterson wrote:

> The plums these days are all going to the writers who can display environments they have long been familiar with in their verisimilar aspects. . . . The Midwest has been studied pessimistically; the Midwest has been studied optimistically. Let us now study the Midwest more closely and dispassionately and allow the winters to be no colder than a reputable thermometer registers them to be, the sandstorms no denser, the skies no brighter, and the men and women no more tolerant, no more intolerant than they are. Let's have done with attitudes toward and beatitudes about the Midwest. Fortunately, our own writers have, for the most part, thus written—and we are able to throw stones from the ox-cart with busy joy.

This devotion to reality does not imply, on the part of the regional little magazine, that undiscriminating sort of photographic portrayal which is identified with naturalism. The regionalist is usually selective; he chooses deliberately and carefully those details best suited to the fulfillment of his purpose. It follows that as his general purpose is the definition of a unique region, he will select as his materials those aspects of the region which best define it, those which make it unique. And as a consequence of this exploitation of the unique we find the second general characteristic of midwestern regionalism as displayed in the early *Schooner,* its historical preoccupation.

A hundred, or even fifty, years before the *Schooner* was founded, when the nation was divided into reasonably well defined compartments, the writer interested in exploiting his own region's individuality had no cause to go outside his own time; there were plenty of distinctly regional materials in his contemporary environment to distinguish the region of which he wrote. The Nebraskan, for example, differed from his eastern relative in the problems he faced, the recreations he enjoyed, the clothes he wore, the food he ate, the job at which he worked. With the passage of time and the growth of a greater nationalism, however, these regional peculiarities became less marked. They had not, to be sure, disappeared completely by 1927; but the midwestern writer intent on building a literature around the distinctive aspects of his region found it convenient to revert to an age in which the distinctions were not so subtle.

Historical emphasis is evident in the fiction published by the regional *Prairie Schooner* from its very first page, on which begins Marie Macumber's "The Vine," the story of a sensitive bride from Indiana who is driven insane by the brutal environment of the pioneer plains. Of the seventy-six stories printed by the *Schooner* during its first five years, thirty are laid in a time sufficiently removed to be called historical.

Allied with this historical preoccupation is the third aspect of midwestern regionalism as displayed in the *Prairie Schooner,* its emphasis on natural environment. The Great Plains are, of course, climatically and topographically different from the Atlantic Coast or the Rocky Mountains. But that fact taken alone would be sufficient to support only a few lyric poems, not a literary movement. The fact which lends natural environment its importance to midwestern regionalism is the part that it did play (and to a lesser extent continues to play) in the life of the region. Struggle is the essence of most serious prose. And the constant antagonist of the Nebraska pioneer was nature—interminable distances which could kill a team of oxen; unbroken droughts and baking sun which could destroy a season's crops; sudden furious blizzards which could catch and freeze a man before he reached shelter; raging gales which, unimpeded by hills or trees, gathered force enough to topple a barn. The midwestern pioneer lived from the land and fought nature for his living. While the eastern industrial worker was fighting the early battles of wages and hours and factory conditions, the midwesterner was fighting, just as earnestly, the battles of land and distance and weather.

One need read no more than the first volume of the *Prairie Schooner* to discover the important role which such natural elements play in midwestern regionalism. They are treated factually in such essays as George Jackson's "Cyclone Yarns" and Victoria Samuel's "The Drouth of 1894." They bulk heavily in the poetry: Gilbert Doane's "Arizona Studies," Elizabeth Wittman's "Spring Dawn," A. Ehrenberger's "Sunrise on the Platte," Willis Hudspeth's "A Prairie Schooner," Ruth Flanders' "To the Missouri River." But they assume perhaps their greatest importance in the prose fiction. There nature is not a part of the setting for the action, but a part of the action, assuming the role of a major character. In Marie Macumber's "The Vine" it is drought that moves the story; in Wimberly's "Dispossessed" it is snow; and in Ivan Hall's story it is "Dust."

Because so much of midwestern regional literature as displayed in the *Schooner* revolves around a conflict with the natural elements, that literature tends toward a starkness often pessimistic and at times fatalistic. The battle of the industrial worker or the subjugated race can conceivably be won; at least writers treating those battles can point to the weapons with which victory would be achieved, or write rationally of the utopias which victory would bring. And those writers can endow their characters with a positive optimism based on their hopes of someday controlling the elements which oppress them. But the antagonist of the midwestern pioneer was not to be conquered by emotional appeal or argumentation, education, litigation, or force. The resultant grimness, a fourth characteristic of the *Schooner*'s regionalism, is again especially evident in its fiction.

Before the *Schooner* was two years old, readers fond of the happy ending were complaining of its starkness. Wimberly wrote in the "Ox Cart" for Winter, 1929:

> Our short-story writers number five, and all of them, with the exception, possibly, of Bobette Sellerier, with her "Jade Earrings," run more or less to the ponderous and sober in theme. The *Schooner* has already been accused of catering to tragic stuff. I believe it was Mark Levings, Omaha architect, who said that the pioneers of Nebraska must have had a devil of a time of it if we are to believe what the writers say about them.

Certainly the issue in which Wimberly wrote those remarks is filled with "tragic stuff." Its five stories offer the reader three deaths. Two characters go insane and at least two others come dangerously close to insanity. The central figure of Wimberly's "Tall and Straight" is a physical grotesque; that of Marie Macumber's "Dumb Cattle," an ugly and unloved child.

The following issue devoted over two pages in the "Ox Cart" to a consideration of the *Schooner*'s apparent preoccupation with "death and gloom" and to the readers' criticism of that preoccupation. Included is a long and apparently typical letter from a woman in Chicago:

> I just called my husband at the office to ask him if
> he thought a blanket of white roses or a spray of calla-
> lilies, sent in your care, would be most effective for the
> *Prairie Schooner.* . . . Your gay-covered, and hence
> hopeful-appearing, *Prairie Schooner* arrived just as we
> had finished breakfast, and I sat down immediately, as
> I always do, and read it through. Heavens! what a mor-
> bid affair! I felt so happy when I got up this morn-
> ing; the sun was shining—a rare event in Chicago—and
> now I feel as if the Yoke of the Oxen were around my
> neck. Aren't you happy out in Nebraska? . . . At least do
> your bit toward encouraging a belief in Browning's
> philosophy that "God's in his heaven, all's right with
> the world."

There is interpolated at this point an editorial reply which
indicates that the editors did not regard such pessimism as a
violation of the factual realism which Peterson had urged:

> But he seldom is, and it seldom is, at least so far as
> the emotions of us westerners are concerned. Working
> for a living, especially on a farm, where the winters are
> approximately eight months long, helps to discourage
> that belief. Do you find it in Ruth Suckow's soil stories,
> or Hamsun's, or *The Long Journey?*

The fifth characteristic of midwestern regionalism as it appears in the early *Schooner,* its strong sense of pride, would
at first appear incompatible with its concentration on the
bitter and gloomy aspects of midwestern life. Yet that sense
of pride is recognizable in the very *fact* of regionalism. It is
largely pride—an injured pride—that demands a market for
midwestern writers who presumably possess talents unrecog-
nized by eastern editors. And it is regional pride that com-
missions the writer or editor to delineate his region and to
distinguish it by making it the subject of literature.

But the midwestern regionalist's pride is more than just a
pride in his region's artists or its geographical uniqueness. It
is, strangely, a pride deriving from those very elements which

give his literature its prevailing gloom—the force of the Midwest's winters, the strength of its winds, the vastness of its space, the uncertainty of its crops. Anyone who has watched the octogenarian's eyes flash as he recalls terrifying tales of the "Blizzard of '88" or who has heard the younger Nebraskan's voice swagger through details of the dust storms of the 1930's and the blizzard of 1949 will recognize the nature of this pride, and will detect its presence in the pages of the early *Schooner*. He who lived through the blizzard of 1888 will, despite recorded data to the contrary, deny that the more recent blizzard was at all comparable in its force. It is the nature of his pride that he should do so. For the peculiar regional pride of the midwesterner attaches not to advantages but to disadvantages overcome. The plainsman does not gloat over the extent of his region's progress; he recognizes that culturally and industrially his region lags behind the nation's longer-settled areas. He does gloat over the fact that any progress, or even survival, has been possible in the face of his region's natural obstacles; hence the greater those obstacles can be made to appear, the greater his satisfaction. The misery in those stories which won the *Schooner* its early reputation for gloom— the frequent emphasis on those who succumbed—is a symptom of the peculiar regional pride of those who survived.

The midwestern regional pride is, of course, more often implicit in the *Schooner*'s contents than stated. The fullest statement of the midwestern point of view was written not by a Nebraskan but by a resident of New York, Benjamin Appel. In an article "Easterners and the Middle West" (Summer, 1931), Mr. Appel, who had not yet achieved his reputation as a writer of fiction, wrote quite convincingly his charge that the "Eastern savage" completely fails to understand or appreciate the beauty and virtues of the Great Plains.

The article must have been gleefully received by many of the *Schooner*'s subscribers. For, by reason of its essentially negative nature, the midwestern regional pride is inclined to be sensitive and somewhat pugnacious. An easterner who fails to recognize the Midwest's struggle (the immensity of its obstacles and the short period in which it has tried to overcome them) and who points to its cultural lag as the ultimate fact is sure to be greeted with injured indignation. Such indignation does not fit gracefully into the editorial pages of a literary little magazine, but on at least one occasion, when the attacker was a former Nebraskan who had deserted to the opposing camp, the *Schooner* vented its rage. In the short-lived editorial column "Dog in the Manger," Wilbur Gaffney wrote (Winter, 1929, p. 76):

> I have just been belatedly reading *Youth and the Bright Medusa,* by Willa Cather. Unless you are one of these people who think our part of the West is full of Main Streets and dull Main Street people, I shouldn't advise reading it. She takes up page after page weeping (figuratively speaking) about how dull and without art-consciousness life in Pittsburgh and Columbus, Ohio, and Red Oak, Iowa, and Broken Bow [Nebraska] is to a person of any artistic sensitiveness. Willa Cather herself lived for a number of years in Bank Street, in Greenwich Village, New York. The Village itself isn't any too inspiring a place; but I've seen Bank Street in my time, and I hardly think Miss Cather is in a position to run down the esthetic possibilities of towns in the West.

Without questioning its moral justification or even its accuracy, one must describe that statement as more emotive than rational. It is an extreme display of that regional pride which, together with a factual realism, a historical preoccupation, an emphasis on natural environment, and a pessimistic starkness, serves to characterize midwestern regionalism as displayed in the early *Prairie Schooner.*

Such severely regionalistic expression probably does little damage to a magazine which is, like a house organ or a political party letter, circulated only among friends. And that the *Schooner* so regarded itself at the beginning of its third year is suggested, unconsciously perhaps, by the treatment of place names in the above editorial statement. Although Gaffney felt compelled to identify Columbus, Ohio, and Red Oak, Iowa, by giving their states, he didn't feel it necessary to write "Nebraska" after Broken Bow. Yet Broken Bow had at the time a population of only about 2,500 and would hardly have been known outside the state.

Had the *Prairie Schooner* remained primarily a magazine for Nebraska writers and Nebraska readers, it might possibly have run its entire course under a stringent and narrow regional policy, with its several restrictions. But, as we have seen, the *Schooner* soon began to attract notice outside its regional boundaries. During its first three years the name of the *Prairie Schooner,* and copies of it, circulated far beyond the borders of Nebraska and even of the Midwest.

The results were inevitable; American writers interested in publishing are not long to seek out new potential markets. So, although most of the material for the first issue of the *Schooner* had been solicited on the campus, issue by issue more and more unsolicited contributions arrived through the mail, many of them from points far from Lincoln.

This influx of contributions from outside the Midwest created for the *Schooner* an editorial dilemma. Its announcement of publication still described it as "an outlet for literary work in the University of Nebraska and a medium for the publication of the finest writing of the prairie country." Yet with the *Schooner*'s first success, Nebraskans and other midwestern writers found themselves competing for space against an increasing number of "outside" contributors. As viewed practically by Wimberly and his associates, the dilemma represented a choice between encouraging writers from the limited area by printing their works, often to the exclusion of superior material from outside the area, or printing the best manuscripts received irrespective of place of origin and thus sacrificing much of the regional tone.

Wimberly's decision is revealed in the magazine's contents. The first issue was almost exclusively a campus project. In the issue for Spring, 1929, the published contributions from outside the university exceeded, for the first time, those from the staff and student body. With the Summer issue of that year, Lincolnites among the contributors were outnumbered by those from outside the city. A year later, in the number for Summer, 1930, Nebraskans were in the minority in a table of contents which included writers from Wisconsin, Maryland, Florida, New York, and Mexico. And the issue for Spring, 1931 carried the work of six writers from the Midwest and eleven writers from outside that region.[2]

It is evident that the *Schooner* had yielded to the attraction of publishable manuscripts received from beyond the region which it had originally adopted as its special province. The new attitude was specifically announced by Wimberly in the "Ox Cart" for Spring, 1935:

> The *Schooner* editors have . . . been charged with discriminating against the home-town writer—the home-town in this case being Lincoln, Nebraska. Or they are said to favor such a writer to the exclusion of an author who may be handicapped by living in such remote places as Peoria, Illinois, Brattleboro, Vermont, or Walla Walla, Washington. As a matter of fact, though, the geographical habitat of a writer is never permitted to sway the sturdy judgment of the *Schooner* editors, even when the writer's manuscript bears such an address as Singapore, Xochimilco, or Bannockburn.

[2] The term "Midwest" is here defined, as by John T. Flanagan, *America Is West* (Minneapolis, 1945, p. iii), to include the twelve states Ohio, Indiana, Illinois, Michigan, Wisconsin, Minnesota, Iowa, Missouri, Nebraska, Kansas, and the Dakotas. But even if one extends the *Schooner's* proper regional territory to include Wyoming, Colorado, Montana, and Oklahoma, the "outside" contributions to this issue of the *Schooner* still exceed those from within the region.

To those few who still carry the word "Regionalism" as a banner, the *Schooner*'s discarding of stringent regional restrictions may appear to have been a "selling out," an abandoning of its original worthy cause. If so, the *Schooner* was not the first such offender; the other leading midwestern little magazine had already extended its scope. John T. Frederick had written, in the *Midland* for January-February, 1930: "With this issue of *The Midland* the phrase 'a national literary magazine' replaces 'a magazine of the Middle West' on the cover and title page. This is in somewhat belated recognition of the fact that almost from the beginning the material printed in the magazine has come from all parts of the country."

But apart from that, close consideration suggests that the *Schooner*'s course of action in broadening its sphere was consistent with its original purpose, that it was the inevitable alternative to literary suicide, and further, that the choice was in the best interests not only of the *Schooner* but of the midwestern writer and of the nation's literature.

The *Schooner* had been founded largely to fill what was felt to be a void in the American publishing structure. That there had been a need for a literary outlet catering to midwestern writers is clearly suggested by the number of midwestern writers who, over the years, have been discovered or encouraged by the *Schooner*. That the writing thus fostered was worth while is indicated by the early success achieved by the *Schooner* itself and by the success of many midwestern writers promoted through its pages. But the founders of the *Schooner*, in offering the midwestern writer a market, had no wild dreams of moving the literary center of the United States to Lincoln, Nebraska, or even of establishing a second center to compete with the New York-Philadelphia-Boston area. They knew, of course, that the East, with its concentration of population, its abundance of magazines, and its virtual monopoly on commercial book publication, would remain the clearing house for the nation's literary reputations. The *Schooner*'s practical function as a market for midwestern writers was primarily to bring good writers to the attention of the eastern publishers. Having done so, the *Schooner* usually lost those writers to the more attractive eastern market. As Wimberly commented in the "Ox Cart" of the *Schooner* for Summer, 1937, "The history of the little magazine is . . . a chronicle of author-finding and author-losing. To edit such a periodical is somewhat like prospecting for gold—starting out with a poor grubstake, then finding pay dirt only to have somebody jump one's claim."

The rueful tone of Wimberly's statement was perhaps conditioned by the financial difficulties which the *Schooner* was experiencing at the time. As later chapters will show, he has worked unselfishly to boost authors from the *Schooner* to a wider and financially rewarding market. The obvious danger of the process is that by losing its choice contributors the *Schooner* might decline in quality to the extent that, even if it did not collapse, it would no longer be an effective medium for the author's progress.

There seemed but two conceivable methods of avoiding that fatal decline: one was through gaining access to an interminable stream of good new midwestern writers; the other was through extending the scope of the *Schooner* to include writing of quality from outside the Midwest. Had the first course been open to him, Wimberly would have preferred it; but it proved only hypothetical. After its early success, the *Schooner* was heavily showered with manuscripts from midwesterners, especially from Nebraskans: university students ambitious to see their names in print; high school girls who had already published "poems" in their school paper; aging settlers who, attracted by the magazine's title, recounted pioneer yarns; relatives and home-town friends of writers whose work had met with success in the *Schooner* office. Some of these people showed promise and were encouraged; a few of the contributions were publishable and appeared; but an overwhelming majority of the manuscripts were totally unacceptable to a magazine anxious about its standards and its future. When the inferior had been culled, there remained not nearly enough to fill the pages left blank by the Macumbers, Eiseleys, and Magarets who were now marketing their literary output in the East.

Luckily for the *Schooner,* and for those writers who through it obtained their earliest success, the second course of action, that of accepting worthwhile material from outside the limits of the Midwest, existed in fact. The increasing flow of manuscripts from "outside" brought much that Wimberly was happy to print. By the time the *Schooner* was five years old, its pages had carried work by such competent writers as Roderick Lull from Oregon, Norman Macleod from Arizona, Jesse Stuart from Kentucky, José Garcia Villa from New Mexico, Kemp Malone from Maryland, William March and Harold Vinal from New York City.

By publishing contributions from such writers as those in preference to inferior writings by midwesterners, Wimberly helped insure the quality and hence the reputation of the *Schooner.* In so doing, he also rendered a valuable service to capable midwestern authors who were publishing their early efforts in the *Schooner;* for the better the magazine in which he published, the better the unknown writer's chance of making an impression where it counts.

But the lowering of the regional bar had even greater implications. The founders of the *Schooner* had recognized the midwestern writer's need for a literary market; perhaps they had failed to recognize that the need for an outlet was not peculiar to midwestern writers. Certainly, however, the experiences of the *Schooner*'s early years suggested that the publishing difficulty faced by the unknown midwestern writer existed not because he was midwestern but because he was unknown. Midwestern writers who had proved themselves in the *Schooner* were accepted and even sought by the commercial publishers of the East.[3] At the same time, the flood of publishable manuscripts from eastern and far-western writers indicated the commercial publishers' unwillingness to take a chance on *any* unknown writer, regardless of the region he represented. The situation has been well described by Hoffman:

> The commercial publishers—the large publishing houses and the big "quality magazines"—are the rear guard. In a few instances they are the rear guard because their editors are conservative in taste, slow to recognize good new writing; but more frequently the commercial publishers are the rear guard because their editors will accept a writer only after the advance guard has proved that he is, or can be made, commercially profitable. Whatever the reason for their backwardness, few commercial houses or magazines of the past thirty years can claim the honor of having served the advance guard banner: they have discovered and sponsored only about 20 per cent of our post-1912 writers. . . .[4]

It would have been the worst kind of regionalism—provincialism—for the *Prairie Schooner* to have ignored the real situation once that situation was apparent. On the other hand, by offering space to writers on the basis of their talent rather than of their address or choice of setting, the *Schooner* assumed a role far greater and more significant than that which it originally undertook.

There were, then, ample practical reasons for the *Schooner*'s abandoning of stringent regionalism. Its relaxing of regional restrictions operated to the benefit of the magazine itself, and of all competent writers in search of a market. But

---

[3] Margaret Christie, literary agent, wrote to Marie Macumber on July 29, 1929: "A long talk with Mr. Hewitt Howland, editor of Century, shows him to be very interested in the work of young writers in general, and midwesterners in particular." See also Helene Margaret's report, pp. 37-38.

[4] Hoffman, *op. cit.*, p. 3.

there was a deeper and broader justification for the change in policy. Wimberly decided, by 1930, that midwestern regionalism as a conscious literary motive was anachronistic. He has publicly expressed that conclusion, and the reasons underlying it, on three occasions: once in a paper on "Regional Literature" read at the convention of the National Association of Teachers of English, in Cleveland, November 29, 1930; again in an editorial, "The New Regionalism," in the *Schooner* for Summer, 1932; and finally in an article for the Chicago *Sun Book Week,* December 2, 1945. Wimberly's conclusions have evoked cries of treason from those who still regard regionalism as a vital literary movement, but it is difficult to quarrel with his logic.

The evidence on which Wimberly bases his argument is a matter of historic record; regional distinctions are becoming increasingly less pronounced. Under the pressure of increasing travel, improved communication, mass production and distribution, federal controls, and standardized education, Americans have become primarily national- rather than regional-minded. The effect of this fact on regional art is pointed out in Wimberly's article for *Book Week*:

> Like other writers, the regional author must find his materials in man's thinking, feeling and acting. But what if man here in America is ceasing to act regionally, so to speak, and is coming more and more to conduct himself in terms of a broad national culture? In so far as they conform to national patterns, our dress, our speech, our manners, and our morals cannot supply the writer with the materials of a local or special way of life.[5]

---

[5] *Cf.* Malcolm Cowley, *Exile's Return,* New York, 1951, pp. 4-5: "Sectional and local influences were relatively more important during the years before 1900 . . . . [After 1900] regional traditions were dying out; all regions were being transformed into a great unified market for motorcars and Ivory soap and ready-to-wear clothes. The process continued during the childhood of the new generation of writers. Whether they grew up

To write authentically with any real regional emphasis, then, the midwestern author is tempted to do what was obviously typical of the regional efforts in the early *Schooner*—move his setting back to a time when regional distinctions were genuine and pronounced. But there is a limit to the number of ways in which writers can tell the story of the great blizzard or the drought-stricken crop or the Indian encounter. Or, if there be no limit to the ways of telling, there is a limit to the number of such stories an intelligent reader living in an industrial society will read.

Regionalism of the type displayed in the early *Schooner,* in which portrayal of the region often seemed the dominant purpose, was wearing thin by the 1930's. W. O. Clough, in an article entitled "Regionalism" which appeared in one of the most clearly regional of American magazines, the *Rocky Mountain Review* (Winter, 1938-39), stated the case brilliantly:

> . . . There is a certain danger in a too great insistence on the regional, for the best writing will always be found to contain universal notes as well. The too conscious effort to be regional is apt to distract the younger writer into artificiality, or into straining for what are, after all, secondary effects. The important thing is character, truth to men and women, wherever they live. Egdon Heath, for example, is a region and Hardy's folks are regional. But the power of the novel is not that it is regional, but that it sets off man against nature in

in New England, the Midwest, the Southwest or on the Pacific Coast, their environment was almost the same; it was a little different in the Old South, which had kept some of its local manners but was losing them. The childhood of these writers was less affected by geography than it was by the financial situation of their parents, yet even that was fairly uniform . . . . All but a handful were pupils in the public schools, where they studied the same textbooks, sang the same songs and revolted rather tamely against the same restrictions. At the colleges they attended, usually some distance from their homes, they were divested of their local peculiarities, taught to speak a standardized American English and introduced to the world of international learning." Note that Cowley is describing America as he experienced it more than a generation ago.

terms of a universal conflict. The regional element is, in one sense, little more than stage setting, the concentration of a cosmic problem into a narrowed focus, for the sake of heightened intensity. The region gains its importance from the greater issues.

The point, finally, is that the term "regional" should be used sparingly. The sensitive, intelligent writer, honestly endeavoring to say what he has to say, will reveal his origins, even against his intention. The regional will take care of itself, for if it is genuine, it will be at least half unconscious, unplanned.[6]

It has been Wimberly's experience that most of the better writers of the past twenty years have preferred to concentrate on the more nearly universal, rather than to stake their reputations on the importance or permanence of the consciously regional. In his article for *Book Week,* he commented on that fact:

> It is not that the "little" magazines do not welcome regional writings. It is simply that such writings do not, in any noticeable quantity, come their way. *Prairie Schooner* is called a regional magazine. Its editors select their material from some 2,500 manuscripts a year, but they are lucky if in the course of a year they find a dozen pieces of authentic regional writing.

In the face of such conditions, it would obviously have been difficult for the *Schooner* to continue successfully as a magazine of midwestern regionalism in the strict sense of that term.

With the issue for Fall, 1940, the *Schooner* dropped from its title page the statement of its being "an outlet for literary work in the University of Nebraska and a medium for the publication of the finest writing of the prairie country." The magazine thus officially abandoned its regional pretensions.

[6] This essay was reprinted in the *Rocky Mountain Reader,* edited by Ray B. West and published by E. P. Dutton in 1946.

As in the case of the *Midland*, the action was belated. If the *Schooner* of the past twenty years can properly be called—as it usually is called—a regional little magazine, it is only after carefully re-defining the word *regional*.

Thus, Charles Allen's appraisal of the *Schooner* fails to recognize changes both in the region and in the magazine:

> The *Prairie Schooner* (1927-) and *The Frontier* (1920-39), have favored a more pessimistic interpretation of their regions than have the Southwestern quarterlies. The *Prairie Schooner*, speaking primarily for the Great Plains and the agricultural Midwest, and *The Frontier*, speaking for the mountains and plateaus of the Pacific Northwest, represent sections that are still largely raw and dreary expanses whose people often are forced to live on an elementary and depressing level. Perhaps the refusal to compromise with the bitter, often brutalizing reality of their regions accounts for the suspicion with which some observers have regarded both magazines.[7]

Conscious emphasis on midwestern regional themes is no longer a characteristic of the *Schooner*. One must, for example, search hard through the more recent volumes to discover a pioneer story or a poetic tribute to the beauties of the plains. One can only assume, then, that Allen's judgment is based on second-hand impressions or remote recollections— that he has never seen the rancher from western Nebraska check his stock from his own airplane or send his daughter off to college in a new red Cadillac convertible. Although Nebraska in 1945 ranked only twenty-fifth among the states in average per-capita income, the low cost of living in Nebraska made it possible for the residents to live considerably above an

[7] Hoffman, *op. cit.*, p. 130. The passage in which this comment appears, the first half of Chapter VIII, is an almost verbatim reprint of an article by Allen, "Regionalism and the Little Magazines," *College English*, VII, 10-16 (1945).

"elementary and depressing level." Furthermore, the state ranked second among the forty-eight in literacy, preceded only by its neighbor Iowa. Allen's statement about a "refusal to compromise" is misleading. Not since the early 1930's has bitter and pessimistic regional fiction appeared in any considerable quantity in the *Schooner*.

Indicative of the new attitude toward traditional midwestern regionalism is a group of four parodies by Robert Aldrich, which appeared under the title "Ladies from Nebraska" in the Summer issue of 1942. There Aldrich makes fun not only of four Nebraska novelists (including his mother, Bess Streeter Aldrich) but of the very themes and methods which characterize the conscious regionalism of the earlier *Schooner*. Also indicative of the *Schooner*'s broader scope is the fact that advocates of regions other than the Midwest appear in the magazine frequently: Byron Herbert Reece, Jesse Stuart, LeGarde S. Doughty, Ray B. West, as well as many writers who are not called regional because their peculiar environment happens to be New York City or Boston. Through 1942 and 1943 the *Schooner* cooperated with the Committee on Cultural Relations with Latin America; it was the first magazine to print in English the work of the Mexican poets Octavio Paz and Efraín Huerta. And in 1949 it became active in the International Literary Pool of UNESCO.

Yet in developing from an "outlet for literary work in the University of Nebraska . . ." to a participant in international schemes for the promotion of literature, the *Schooner* has not completely abandoned the writers of the Midwest. To the extent that it can do so without sacrificing literary standards, the *Schooner* has continued in its original purpose of encouraging and developing writers from its immediate region. Its record of service to those writers is a good one. The midwesterner finds, however, that a regional theme is not an infallible key for entry into the *Schooner*'s pages.

5

Editorial Policy: Preferences and Prejudices

Since the *Prairie Schooner* discarded conscious regionalism, its editorial policy has not been one easily characterized by a single term, unless it be that of eclecticism. Lowry C. Wimberly has had final control over the magazine's contents; an attempt to define the *Schooner*'s editorial policy is, therefore, essentially a study of his editorial tastes as revealed in the material which he selects for publication.

At the base of Wimberly's editorial judgment lies his conception of what the *Schooner*'s appeal should be. And in this fundamental consideration the *Schooner*'s policy is different from that of many another little magazine. Those magazines which represent a particular political or critical school customarily direct their publications at a select group of fellow members in that school, so that the writers whom they publish are communicating with an audience composed largely of fellow authors and sympathetic critics. But since abandoning regionalism, the *Schooner* has not allied itself with any such school. In gauging reader reaction to any manuscript under consideration, Wimberly anticipates an assorted audience— not, of course, an intellectual cross-section of America, but an adult audience of better than average intelligence and with a more than average sympathy for, and understanding of, literature. It is that audience, Wimberly feels, which will be the final arbiter of all literary reputations, not only for little magazines but, more important, for the thousands of writers who use the little magazine to gain practice and prestige for a wider future literary success.

Having fixed upon that audience, Wimberly has done his best to give it material that is interesting and varied. He has attempted always to avoid what is either dull or consciously esoteric. And above all he has insisted that the *Schooner* remain primarily a vehicle for creative writing rather than for social, political, or critical discussion. He deplores the tendency of America's magazines to turn from literature proper to publishing primarily treatises and essays and learned articles. In the issue for Winter, 1935, he attributed the unpublished writer's plight largely to the fact that reputable magazines had ceased publishing literature in favor of such prose:

> It is chiefly by courtesy, one feels, that certain magazines are, nowadays, called "literary" or that they are placed in the "quality" group of periodicals. I am thinking specifically of magazines like the *Atlantic* and *Harper's*. And I am assuming, of course, that a magazine is to be called "literary" only as it allots generous space in each issue to stories and poems of a high order or to essays, sketches, and, perhaps, biography, or an occasional play. But as a matter of fact such periodicals as *Harper's* or the *Atlantic,* as well as *Scribner's* and the *Mercury,* and, so too, the *Forum,* are extremely niggardly with their space so far as literary or artistic writings are concerned. I haven't time here to be statistical, but if any *Schooner* reader will glance at the contents of the leading "quality" magazines he will find listed something like eight articles for every story, and, if he looks closely, he may find a poem or two, included for reasons of magazine format or by a sort of typographical chance or by the grace of God. But it seems that art has generally fared thus in our busy, fact-enslaved world.

In attempting to avoid that observed error of the "quality" magazines, Wimberly has maintained in his selection of material a balance which favors the purely creative. The one hundred issues covering the *Schooner*'s first twenty-five years have carried 602 pieces of prose fiction (short stories, short-shorts, and fictional sketches), 1,264 poems, 8 plays, and only 349 pieces of non-fiction prose (informative articles and essays ranging from the highly personal to the generally philosophical.[1] To the degree that availability of good manuscripts and space has allowed, Wimberly has attempted to keep approximately that balance in each issue of the *Schooner*. Only three times has the *Schooner* failed to carry contributions representing all three major types of writing, fiction, expository prose, and poetry; two consecutive issues in the year 1933 (both severely abbreviated depression numbers) and one issue in 1937 contained no non-fiction prose.

Whether or not the individual writer's manuscript is accepted for publication in the *Schooner* depends largely upon the number of other manuscripts in the same genre against which it is competing. Manuscripts which are rejected, over 95 per cent of those submitted, fail because they do not, in competition with other manuscripts of their type, sufficiently measure up to standards which Wimberly has adopted through a lifetime of studying and working with literature. Or, to phrase the same matter from the point of view of the disappointed writers of the unsuccessful manuscripts, they fail because they do not sufficiently anticipate Wimberly's editorial preferences and prejudices.

One general quality which Wimberly seeks in all manuscripts is "honesty." This quality, which is difficult to define

[1] The figures presented here exclude regular editorial features, for which see pp. 104-106. One wonders at Allen's statement in Hoffman, *op. cit.*, p. 138: "With the exception of *The Midland* and *The Prairie Schooner,* the regional periodicals have published a good many essays and articles . . . ." The 349 carried by the *Schooner* would seem "a good many."

or discuss but which most literary critics profess an ability to recognize, has to do with the writer's being true to himself. It denies the author's right to go outside his physical or mental experience, or to adopt an unnatural or distasteful attitude for the sake of a literary effect, or to force his statements into words or phrases which are not essentially his own. Wimberly has expressed the requirement thus (Fall, 1946, 231):

> A writer . . . should recognize his inborn and acquired limits, should not attempt to be a T. S. Eliot (as who wants to be?) when congenitally he is an Edgar Guest. Or if he believes in the Republican Party, monogamy, the sanctity of marriage, the sacredness of parenthood, the fickleness of blondes, is down on intoxicating liquor or even strong coffee or coffee weak or strong, and contends that Van Johnson isn't a ham actor, he can write convincingly only within the confines of his beliefs. If he is a born sentimentalist he must write sentimental stuff and not attempt satire. He must depict all children as little angels and all old men as hoary-headed saints. He must view all men as naturally good, and should keep handy a tub of whitewash wherewith to whiten all the villains, if, that is, in a cynical moment, he concedes that there are villains abroad in the land. And if he spots a wolf here and there he should dress it out in sheep's clothing.
>
> In other words, as the unique being—ass or wise man —that he is, a writer can be successful only in so far as he expresses, whether in drama, poetry, or fiction, his own peculiar brand of asininity or of wisdom.

Other general requirements which Wimberly imposes upon his contributors mark him by the standards of such little magazines as *VVV, Furioso,* or even *Accent,* as a conservative. Wimberly insists upon intelligibility and upon clean, clear, careful writing. He distrusts the severely cryptic, and he has little sympathy for private systems of grammar, syntax, or punctuation. And if in his requirements on this score he runs somewhat behind, or perpendicular to, recent little-magazine

tradition, it is not without his own awareness of the fact. In
the Spring issue for 1946 (p. 68), he wrote:

> . . . The *Schooner* has always shied away from innova-
> tion and experimentation. It still holds, for instance,
> to such outworn practices as printing lucid prose and
> not wholly unintelligible verse. And it continues to
> begin sentences with capital letters, to end them with
> the orthodox marks of punctuation, and to make a dis-
> tinction between a dash and a semicolon or, again, a
> dash and a colon or, yet once more, between a dash and
> a row of dots.

Wimberly does not, then, resent the charge of conservatism
in these matters. He envisions an ultimate vindication, for
he feels that the true road of American literature is the one
which he and the *Schooner* are following, and that the more
extreme little magazines are on a side path which will lead
them either to destruction or gradually back around to a meeting with the *Schooner* on the main road.

But to understand fully the basis for Wimberly's editorial
decisions it is necessary to go far beneath such general attitudes
and examine more specifically his opinions on each of the
three literary forms: fiction, poetry, and non-fiction prose.

The *Schooner* prints, on the average, about six pieces of
fiction per issue. In selecting that fiction, Wimberly generally
favors the short story of between two thousand and five thousand words. It has been his observation that only rarely can a
writer achieve a significant effect in fewer than two thousand
words, and that stories of over five thousand words are seldom
economical in their development—that they usually contain
padding, the removal of which not only makes a story of more
convenient length but also increases its dramatic effect.

This padding he most frequently finds at the two crucial
points of the story: the beginning, where the author may lose
his reader, and the end, where he may lose his effect on the

reader. Frequently manuscripts which were at first unacceptable because of such padding have been printed after
a simple cutting of the objectionable material. Thus Mark
Schorer was asked to eliminate an "unnecessary preamble" before his excellent story "Minna Is Left Alone" (Summer, 1933)
was published. And in the original manuscript of William
Ornstein's "Dutchman's Britches in a Blue Sky" (Winter,
1946), five pages of background material preceded the first
word of the story as it was finally published.

Even more frequently than the "unnecessary preamble,"
Wimberly finds the weakening superfluity at the end of—or,
more properly, beyond the end of—the story. Ercelle Davis'
story "Not In the Record" was published (Winter, 1947) after
the omission of the last paragraph, and Mary Ormsbee Whitton's "For Ever and Ever, Amen" (Fall, 1944) after the omission of the next to the last. And after receiving Wimberly's
criticism of "Conversation Piece" (Summer, 1946), Ralph
Steele wrote: "Since 'Conversation Piece' was originally written to end at the place you indicate, it is perfectly agreeable
to me to return it to its original state. The later part was
probably just the word-slinging urge and should have been cut
away before the piece was sent out. Thank you for seeing
the spot it should end."

Although some endings can be thus repaired to Wimberly's
satisfaction, most of the stories returned because of weak endings (and there are many) are not cases for a simple excision.
More often the difficulty involves internal structural weakness.
Wimberly's attitude toward the short story is essentially the
classic one attributed to Poe. He is most favorably disposed
toward that story which builds toward a high point of interest,
a climax, followed by a swift but clear denouement. And, like
Poe, he insists that the outcome of the story be plausibly
motivated and consistent with that which has gone before.
Solutions which derive from accident or which cannot be explained in terms of the preceding action are regarded un-

favorably. Changes in character must result from causes apparent to the reader rather than simply from the desires of the author.

Evidence of Wimberly's insistence upon careful motivation and his preference for climactic order are again to be found in the comments of contributors whose manuscripts were revised before winning Wimberly's acceptance. Venard McLaughlin wrote of his story "The Man Who Ran" (Spring, 1941): "Again thanks for help on this story. Following your suggestion I've added another motivating incident. . . . The incident selected seems . . . to be also a natural outgrowth of the story with specific plants on pages three and four." Paul Ellerbe wrote, on resubmitting his "Lady Writer" (Spring, 1945):

> I have at last got around to acting on the suggestion you made back in July: ". . . you need to make it clear just how such a woman could 'grow up.'" You said if I could show that by revising the ending, you'd like to read it again, and suggested that perhaps an incident of some sort would turn the trick. I have sought for such an incident and I'll be grateful if you'll see if you think the trick has been turned.

Similar letters cover the revisions of Hal Ellson's first *Schooner* contribution, "The Great Orchestra" (Fall, 1936), Frank Brookhouser's "Brother Bill and Janie" (Winter, 1940) and again his "No Girls to Kiss in Gutheim" (Spring, 1947), Harold J. Matthews' "Mister Slim" (Spring, 1941), Melville Cane's "Mr. Samuels: Barber" (Fall, 1944), Eileen Shaw's "Ollie" (Fall, 1946), Fred Shaw's "Skirmish at Baytown" (Winter, 1947), and many others.

In addition to his requirements concerning form, Wimberly has shown (as doubtless have all other editors) some predispositions as to the tone and subject matter of the stories he selects.

The *Schooner* has been accused by its readers of "catering to tragic stuff" and by Charles Allen of favoring a generally pessimistic interpretation of the region it represents.[2] Certainly Wimberly is no Pollyanna. He has often expressed his awareness of the tragedy in life and of the need for its treatment in literature. In one four-hundred-word "Note on Unhappy Endings" (Fall, 1940, 225-226), he wrote:

> If the "little magazines" may be called quality publications it is partly because they are willing to print stories in which the characters—some of them, at least —are permitted to give up the ghost. In other words, these magazines are not afraid of the so-called unhappy ending. The *Schooner* has never rejected a story on the ground that Grandma Smith, central figure in the tale, turned her face to the wall, somewhere in the final paragraph, and breathed her last. Why should the editor mail such a story back to its author? After all, the thing that happened to Grandma was entirely plausible. Moreover, it was in keeping with the tenets of realistic art.

Certainly the pervading gloom and heaviness of the *Schooner,* particularly the early *Schooner,* are undeniable. But that tone reflects the inclinations of the little-magazine contributor more surely than it does those of the *Schooner*'s editor. Once, having received from a woman subscriber an ultimatum theatening termination of her subscription unless the *Schooner* printed a cheerful story within a year, Wimberly wrote (Spring, 1938, 77): "If this subscriber only knew how hard it is to get cheerful stories she might relent a bit and give us two years to find one." That comment is, of course, hyperbolic, but it is only partially in jest. Little magazines, especially those which are called regional, seem naturally to draw fiction which is sombre and heavy. There are many possible explanations for this. Commercial publishers for the most part shy away from

[2]See p. 77.

such material, with the result that the burden of publication is placed on the non-commercial magazines. Furthermore, little-magazine contributors as a group tend to be intellectually sober, thoughtful people who are seriously concerned with the problems of their environment. Then too, while it may not be an immediate influence, the fact that a writer must sometimes work very hard to give away the story which he has worked very hard to produce doubtless fosters a pessimistic view of our society and life in general. And finally, in the case of a magazine identified with midwestern regionalism, as we have seen, the historical and environmental elements tend to dictate a pessimistic tone in those stories which treat of the region.

Whatever the reason behind this preponderance of pessimistic realism in the submissions, Wimberly had barely begun his career as editor before he had observed it as a fact. And realizing that such pessimism is a rut into which the *Schooner* could very easily slip, Wimberly has been constantly on the lookout for stories which will alleviate the heavy tone.

While he will not intentionally sacrifice quality to variety in his choice of fiction, Wimberly is always receptive to stories embodying well written humor or satire. A look through the *Schooner* files will reveal that he finds a considerable amount of it: such stories as Weldon Kees' "Three Pretty Nifty Green Suits" (Winter, 1936), Jacqueline Wright's "Mr. Stover's Pants" (Spring, 1936), Eudora Welty's "Lily Daw and the Three Ladies" (Winter, 1937), Robert Fontaine's "Grandfather and the Widow LaChance" (Winter, 1944), two groups of parodies by Bob Aldrich (Fall, 1941, and Summer, 1942), and several "fables" by William March (Spring, 1941, and Spring, 1942).[3]

In his reaction against the realism with which he has been bombarded, however, Wimberly has not depended entirely

[3] The first three stories named are available in the anthology *Prairie Schooner Caravan* (Lincoln, 1943), as are one group of Aldrich's parodies and six of March's fables.

upon humor and satire. As early as 1929 he wrote (Winter, 1929, 79): "It is high time we were getting away from the 'scientific' realism that has had such a vogue of late years. We like to see a writer who can spin a yarn out of airy nothing and who does not have to do a 'research job' before putting the fictional pen to paper."

One of Wimberly's favorite types of story is that which involves the supernatural or super-normal. His early career in scholarship gave him much knowledge of and sympathy for folklore, including the witch story, the ghost story, and the tale of magic. And he has long been seriously interested in the possibilities and potentialities of telepathy, clairvoyance, prescience, and other branches of parapsychology. As editor, he finds it difficult to reject a well written story in which one or more of those elements are involved. And his own *Schooner* stories "Dispossessed" (April, 1927) and "The Red Gentian" (Spring, 1928) demonstrate his affinity for the super-normal as a device of literature and a relief from pessimistic realism.

Still another type of story which supports Wimberly's re-action against the naturalistic or harshly realistic is that which involves the subjective, non-clinical treatment of normal, pre-ferably happy, emotions. In Wimberly's words (Winter, 1930, 66), "The *Prairie Schooner* . . . may or may not be humanistic, but the editors have tried to keep it human." Among stories of this type in the *Schooner* are Robert Hutchinson's humor-ous-pathetic "Lovely Free Gift" (Winter, 1946), Robert Fon-taine's "Many-Colored Glass" (Summer, 1944), and Chloe Gartner's delightful "Giuseppe Goes Home" (Fall, 1938).

In the note accompanying the last-named story, Wimberly editorially reinforced his desire to alleviate the harsh realism of which the *Schooner* had been accused: "With [Chloe Gart-ner's] story 'Giuseppe Goes Home' the editors hope to initiate the publication of work in the 'romantic mood.' They feel that it is high time that American writers cease to give all their attention to social problems, economic plights, and the manifold, weird dilemmas relating to sex."

A few such editorial statements, when coupled with the normal number of manuscript rejections, lead naturally to a charge that the *Schooner* is operated under a system of strict taboos. There is, however, only one rule in the *Schooner's* editorial code which is inviolable to the extent of being properly called a taboo. This is the rule prohibiting the publication of stories in bad taste. The taboo is most often invoked against stories involving sex or obscenity. Not once in the *Schooner's* history has an issue been suppressed or banned from the mails —an achievement far from unique among little magazines but nonetheless somewhat surprising in a magazine which has run for over a quarter of a century.

In some cases Wimberly's rejection of a manuscript containing a sex theme is based on artistic considerations. A story which contains obscenity or pornography for its own sake— one, that is, in which the totality of the effect derives from the obscene or the salacious, is in Wimberly's opinion a bad story in its conception.

But Wimberly is not blind to the fact that much good and legitimate modern literature not only contains but depends heavily upon a frank treatment of sex. When confronted with such a piece of writing, Wimberly's editorial decision is a matter of practical judgment rather than of literary taste. His own sensibilities are not easily offended. But the existence of the *Schooner* depends upon continued support from its two chief sources of income—the subscribers and the University of Nebraska. Anything which would raise questions of morality serious enough to endanger the continued support from these two sources, Wimberly has declined to publish regardless of its literary quality. Homosexuality and other perversions fall under the general taboo. The act of love may of course be suggested but may not be described. Nor may the story contain intimate anatomical detail or reference to the bodily functions.

Sometimes the objectionable material is so extended or so closely interwoven with the general effect of the story that to remove it would be impossible. In such cases, Wimberly simply returns the manuscript as unacceptable. Thus Wimberly rejected one story despite the fact that he praised the writing as "some of the best we've had in the Prairie Schooner office" and urged the writer to submit other stories which did not "run so much to sex."[4] But frequently the censorable matter is an incidental impediment which can, by careful revision, be eliminated or disguised. Wimberly commented, in the issue for Fall, 1937 (p. 257): " 'Celia' marks George Abbe's first appearance in our pages. Perhaps we should say that before printing 'Celia' we subjected the story to some slight editorial refrigeration." And Desmond Clarke wrote from Dublin, Ireland, on July 18, 1950: "By all means tone down the story 'Spring' to suit your requirements. . . . I am glad you like it, though I am sorry to have overdone the references to 'breasts.' Toning down will in all probabilities improve it."[5]

There are, in addition to sex, other themes which would violate the absolute taboo against stories in bad taste. For example, the line would be drawn against stories which are openly and deliberately blasphemous, or stories designed to instill race hatred, or, at the present moment, stories planned to win active support for the Russian plan of world domination. But fortunately the taboo against such fiction is largely theoretical; it is a comfort to Wimberly and a credit to the American writer of fiction that hardly ever does a manuscript run afoul of this portion of the *Schooner*'s absolute taboo.

Wimberly does receive, however, many stories containing elements which, while not absolute grounds for rejection, are obstacles to publication. This secondary system of relative

[4] Letter, July 23, 1934.

[5] Despite the "refrigeration" and the "toning down," both of these stories when published, drew letters of protest and cancellations of subscriptions.

taboos operates for the most part against stories which are trite or anachronistic in their themes or unduly specialized in their settings. A serious success story of the Horatio Alger type, for example, is likely to be returned; so is any other story which draws the moral that "Virtue is its own reward." Stories of college campus life are at a clear disadvantage, and patriotic stories of war heroism are not favorably received between wars. And, despite the tag of "regionalism" which still clings to the *Schooner,* Wimberly has long ceased to be favorably disposed toward the manuscript which tells again the story of the harrassed sod-buster or the lonesome cow-poke. Stories which by reason of their theme or setting fall into this group of "undesirables" may occasionally be successful; but if so, it is by reason of a compensating freshness in the handling of the material or a redeeming excellence in the quality of the writing.

Worthy of special attention, because of the historical importance of the movement involved, is Wimberly's attitude toward proletarian literature. It has frequently been charged that the proletarian story falls under another one of his taboos. That is not, strictly speaking, the truth. During the 1930's, when the stream of proletarian literature in this country was running its fullest, the *Schooner* devoted space to the fiction of such left-wing writers as Roderick Lull, Albert Halper, Upton Terrell, and Meridel LeSueur, and it printed many stories of social protest by lesser known writers: Robert Whitehead, Miriam Allen deFord, John T. Coffee, Jr., William Randolph Browne, Bennett Wright, Dorothy Dunsing, Charles Alldredge, and others.

Roderick Lull's first published story, "Fidelity" (Winter, 1931), shows how a rich man's soul and character are gradually smothered by the creature comforts that surround him; he loses his sense of purpose, his ideals, and ultimately even the power to love. Miriam Allen deFord's "Pride" (Spring, 1934) views the other end of the social scale. Two people, one an elderly

woman schoolteacher and the other a young girl, suffer pain
and humiliation because they are poor. The teacher counsels
the girl: ". . . Never give in. Learn your place in the world and
learn to fight for your rights in it. Remember that all your
life, and you will see a better day than I shall ever live to
see. . . . The blind shall see, and the lowly shall be exalted,
and the persecuted shall stand shoulder to shoulder for justice.
Pride and courage—we must find them. . . . And solidarity,
Rhea, we must have that too." And Meridel LeSueur's "Salute
to Spring" (Fall, 1938) is as bitter a story of protest as one
would find in any consciously left-wing magazine. In it a
farm couple with much moral courage but no food or money
are pressed by the government for repayment of a feed loan,
suffer a loss in exchanging wheat for flour, and watch their
baby die because they cannot provide adequate medical care
—all within the space of a few hours.

There is no denying that the *Schooner,* in allotting space
to the proletarian cause, has been less generous than such left-
wing organs as the early *Partisan Review, Left Front, Blast,*
or *Anvil,* or even than such less dedicated magazines as Whit
Burnett and Martha Foley's *Story,* Karlton Kelm's *Dubuque
Dial,* or Lee Luke's *Decade of Short Stories.*[6] But this is not
because Wimberly has enforced a real taboo against the literature of protest. In the *Schooner* for Spring, 1935, he defended
himself against that charge and clearly stated his stand on
proletarian literature:

> As regards taboos, the *Schooner* editors have been
> charged with discriminating against the proletarian
> story, but this charge is not well founded. In the first
> place, proletarian fiction is seldom submitted to the
> *Schooner.* In the second place, that which is submitted
> is seldom worth printing. But if, within the next month

[6] See Hoffman, *op. cit.,* pp. 148-169.

or so, the *Schooner* editors find in the mail a good proletarian yarn they will jump at the chance to print it. Their experience has been, however, that nearly all such pieces submitted to them were either poorly written or they lacked authenticity even to the point, at times, of being palpable "fakes."

That statement not only explains Wimberly's attitude toward proletarian literature; it demonstrates again the editorial policy which has controlled the *Schooner*'s fiction for over a quarter of a century. Wimberly has staunchly resisted making the *Schooner* a special organ of any literary movement—even, as has been demonstrated above, the regionalist movement with which it is commonly identified. He has, rather, maintained a policy of eclecticism, taking what he considers the best of the manuscripts received, regardless of their critical or political direction. That perhaps helps to account for the fact that even in 1935, when literary activity was heavy along the proletarian front, the *Schooner* was not receiving much good left-wing fiction. In the *Schooner* the proletarian story, in competition with stories of all other types, had to stand on its merits as fiction. Yet there were many magazines catering primarily to the proletarian; the writer intent upon publication could hardly ignore the mathematical advantage accruing from the proletarian editor's predisposition toward his point of view.

The message in a story of protest has never *per se* been a deterrent to publication in the *Schooner*. But neither has it been a recommendation. And Wimberly was not the first to discover that an over-awareness of message and a concentration on collateral effects often adversely influence the style and development of a story and damage its literary effects. It is with the literary effects of fiction that Wimberly is primarily concerned. It is on his opinions of those effects that he bases his selection of fiction for the *Prairie Schooner*.

The *Schooner* is generally less well known for its verse than for its fiction. Yet it has consistently published poetry from its first issue in 1927, printing on the average twelve or thirteen poems in each number. Wimberly wrote in the issue for Winter, 1932 (pp. 76-77):

> That the *Prairie Schooner* is interested in poets and poetry of a high order is evidenced by its disposition to print verse other than that of the "filler" variety. We are, generally speaking, averse to the very long or book-length poem, but we feel that poetry deserves more space than may be grudgingly accorded to it by an unfilled page of prose.

The space limits imposed upon a poem are, of course, less proscriptive than those applied to a short story. The *Schooner* has published many poems as short as four lines, and it has published poems as long as 192 (Jesse Stuart, "Another April," Spring, 1941, 43-47). Because most poems are by nature terse and close-knit, Wimberly does not often prescribe cuts or structural revisions with an eye toward subsequent publication—though he did, with the poet's permission in each case, delete the entire last line of Sanora Babb's "Spring Wooing" (Winter, 1933) and several lines from R. C. Pitzer's "Voices" (Summer, 1933).

With such exceptions, occasioned by the difference in form, most of the editorial code which governs the *Schooner*'s fiction applies to its poetry. During the *Schooner*'s early years of regionalism, its poetry was heavy with midwestern themes. But in more recent years it has, in poetry as well as in short stories, avoided becoming the servant of a single movement. In the themes of the *Schooner*'s verse, Wimberly has tried to provide his subscribers with a balanced diet—one which includes, incidentally, the proletarian.

The truth of Wimberly's contention that he is not editorially antagonistic toward the theme of left-wing literature but only insistent that literary quality accompany the theme is demonstrated by the large quantity of proletarian poetry which the *Schooner* has carried—poems by Norman Macleod, Kenneth Patchen, August Derleth, Harry Roskolenko, and many others less well known. In 1932 Wimberly gave editorial recognition to the left-wing literary movement (Winter, 77): "In his poem 'A Piece of Bread' William Allen Ward takes cognizance of that side of life which the present depression has brought so sharply to everyone's attention. In its theme, that is, 'A Piece of Bread' may be classed as 'proletarian' literature—a type of writing that is coming rapidly to the fore."

The most telling charge to be leveled against the *Schooner*'s poetry policy, however, concerns its attitude not toward themes but toward techniques. Under the influences of constant experimentation, verse techniques have changed radically during the *Schooner*'s career. Wimberly, with his conservative insistence upon intelligibility, has not pretended to keep pace with all the changes. He wrote in the "Ox Cart" for Winter, 1940: "No inconsiderable part of modern verse belongs to a class of writing that no one can decipher." Many people, on reading the surrealists or the more obscure imagists, would be inclined to agree with that allegation. Furthermore, it is inescapable that frauds have been perpetrated under the broad cloak of experiment in poetry; during the 1940's incoherent nonsense frequently found its way into print. But one is surprised at the specific targets of Wimberly's attack. He has, for example, privately expressed his doubts as to the sincerity or ability of T. S. Eliot. And whereas the editor of an eclectic little magazine cannot well afford to alienate the many writers to whom such opinions would appear heretical, Wimberly has on at least one occasion indicated in print a mild contempt for Eliot.[7] Equally striking was an editorial comment (Winter, 1928, 86), written by Robert Lasch but

[7] See p. 82.

passed by Wimberly, which dismissed with a "snap of the fingers" the whole group of modern poets printed in the Simon & Schuster "Pamphlet Poet" series. (The group included Conrad Aiken, Witter Bynner, H. D., Alfred Kreymbourg, Elinor Wylie, and others.)

Wimberly's private bark has, however, been worse than his editorial bite. The poetry actually printed in the *Schooner* suggests an editorial policy not nearly so conservative as that of some poetry magazines such as the *Journal of American Poetry*, the *American Bard*, or *Wings*. A certain affinity for traditional forms is apparent in the *Schooner*'s presentations. During the years 1928 through 1930, the *Schooner* carried an American folk ballad in nearly every issue, and it has printed a few since then. Among the other poems, the sonnet is much in evidence, and a great deal of the verse is in quatrains. But such modern attributes as economy of sentiment, toughness of imagery, and freedom from poetic diction prevent most of the sonnets from appearing Shellyesque or the quatrains from resembling Longfellow's.

A few samples from a single issue of the *Schooner*, the Winter number of 1946, will demonstrate that Wimberly's conservative attitude toward poetry has been more a parasol than an impenetrable shell.

Harold Vinal's "Mercurial" (p. 311) is in sonnet form, but it is clearly twentieth-century in its technique:

> Quicksilver was his symbol, he was here
> Only an instant and as quickly gone,
> What volatile ichor in his veins ran clear
> As truth we do not know, he fed upon
> Some elfin pabulum because his wit
> Ran like a lightning in his brain, he smote
> The air about him and we saw him flit
> A moment in the sun, a laughing mote.
> Perhaps Titania's wand befuddles those
> Who play with magic, so you may surmise
> We never caught his spirit in repose.

Behind the mirror we could see his eyes
Burning from quicksilver and from that zone,
Peering out at us, rather than our own.

And despite the traditional appearance of the quatrains on
the page, Rosamund Dargan Thomson's "Yet Innocent"
(p. 261) is essentially modern in its imagery, especially in its
subjective interchange of the senses ("hear the frost"):

Air the color of stones, and stone the color of ice;
My subtlest winter, my peace.
Precious lies a mist on the least of days,
Fast silence on the night.

What will come now will come in velvet,
Color of snows, color of close dusk;
Something heavier than the love hour's hush,
Yet innocent, yet blest.

I must be left in slowness now to brood
On these transparencies of ice and air.
Slowly I lift a veiling, peer;
And hear the frost, and muse.

Bernice Slote's "Apothecary Shop" (p. 256), with its
rhymed couplets and regular meter, is less advanced in its
technique than much of her later verse. Nevertheless, one can
easily identify it as the work of a modern poet; its rich sensuous
effect is achieved through cataloguing the unusual and specific.

The way he was going, he could not tarry.
But he told me this, the apothecary:

"My shop has herbs, and bottles that ray
The sun through glass and color my day.
It's an amethyst, gold, vermilion room.
Garnet and green the corners bloom.
Wine and amber and twilight blue—
In separate ways my sight falls through

The mingling smells of—how many woods?
By leaf and by root I've gone down roads
A man will travel. Which do you know?
Bittersweet herb and wild indigo?
I'll show them all. Here's nut-gall (ground),
Boneset, squaw-vine, strewn around.
Yarrow and hemp and Queen of the Meadow,
Wahoo bark and a little Dutch madder.
Have what you wish for healing and dreams
(My shop is timeless and not what it seems).
A pocket of Life Everlasting will be
The only herb I'll take with me.
I'll give you some rue and close my store.
The bottles you'll find of yourself. Explore!"

He was still as death, the apothecary,
But he said all this when they came to bury.

That unconventional form does not bar a poem from Wimberly's favorable consideration is demonstrated by several pieces of free verse in this same issue. One, "Old Steamboat in Autumn" (p. 246), written by Walter Kidd under the pseudonym Conrad Pendleton, contains echoes of Sandburg:

Its wheelwhirl crumbling green silence of water,
Its bow blue-bulging sidles of froth,
the boat unthroats
              lonesome bronze over evening
like an old-day chorus retroubling monotonous stilled
backwaters of memory.
              Chugging a barge of rivets to loud shipyards
that weld strong song in steel under hammer and guttural
                                                                    torch,
close furrowing foam over watery funnels,
by sea-dulled freighters, by piled docks . . . over smoky stars,
the steamboat limps
down the slow flow west round a bend of autumn.

Another, Kathryn Winslow's "Cat" (p. 309), seems clearly in the tradition of the twentieth-century imagists:

The cat's skin flows on sleep
so smooth
his sinews stretch
a counterpane to lie beneath
feigning ease
while the sly pulse leaps at needlenoise
flashed slender in his ear.

In sleep his memory is shouting
look and the taste of mice
with brittle teeth.
In no alarm
he grasps their silken sides
and their pulp eyes soften to the floor.
But then he wakes
to find the hunt his dream.

No motion tells his spasm of defeat
where he lies in his heart's burrowed pose.
His lust sticks in slits of agate
and none
but the tender imagined mice
take notice.

And, as a final example, there is Norman J. Kraeft's poem
"A Particular Edition of 'Leaves of Grass' " (p. 270). In theme
and tone it is similar to Keats's "On First Looking into Chap-
man's Homer"; but there the similarity ends.

O
at never finding it, the volume
with letters lazy and big,
so tastable green its covers
that hardly reading it as book
you hold it rather amid a glorious spilling of words
exploding that anxious thing inside
 (the thing that no one yet has named)
that, which the words in this book
touch.

That poem is not so difficult or obscure as, say, Wallace Stevens or Robert Lowell, but its presence in the *Schooner* belies any representation of Wimberly as an ultra-conservative in matters of poetry.

It has always been part of Wimberly's plan for the *Schooner* that non-fiction prose should take third place, behind fiction and poetry. He early determined that the *Schooner* should remain a magazine devoted to creative literature rather than to history, criticism, sociology, or politics.

Nevertheless the *Schooner,* in its first twenty-five years, has printed a considerable amount of expository prose. In addition to editorial features, a normal issue of the *Schooner* contains two or three contributed essays or articles. Ten issues have carried as many as seven such pieces, and only three have failed to carry any.

During the early years, when the *Schooner* was operating under an announced policy of regionalism, the articles and essays which it carried dealt primarily with midwestern regional themes. Some of these early regional articles were scholarly and informative, as for example John D. Hick's "Our Pioneer Heritage" (Winter, 1928), an excellent historical interpretation of the region based on Turner's *Significance of the Frontier in American History*. Other contributions, such as Nellie Jane Compton's "Pan of the Prairies" (January, 1927), seemed designed to alleviate the pessimism and harshness attaching to the fictional interpretations of the region by extolling the physical beauty of the Midwest.

The influence of regionalism on the *Schooner*'s early prose is apparent also in a series of critical articles under the general title "Midwestern Writers." The series opened in the *Schooner*'s first issue, in which Bess Streeter Aldrich discussed herself. The next two issues contained articles on two other Nebraskans: Willa Cather (by Robert N. Lasch) and John G. Neihardt (by Russell T. Prescott). In subsequent numbers various *Schooner* contributors treated such midwestern writers as Carl Sandburg, Hamlin Garland, Ruth Suckow, Herbert Quick, Edwin Ford Piper, Ole Edward Rolvaag, Sherwood Anderson, Glenway Wescott, and (again) Willa Cather and Bess Streeter Aldrich. The series continued, with occasional interruptions, until Winter, 1932.

In one respect the *Schooner* has shown more vestiges of regionalism in its expository prose than in its fiction or poetry. It has continued to draw heavily from local writers. Of 247 contributors of non-fiction prose printed by the *Schooner* during its first twenty-five years, 150 have been Nebraskans. The proportion far exceeds that among contributors of fiction or poetry. This, however, has been not so much by choice as by necessity.

The market for articles and essays is considerably different from that for poetry and fiction. For one thing, the paying magazines are on the whole more receptive to non-fiction prose than to belles-lettres; so the need for the little magazine is less. For another, writers interested in making the pages of commercial magazines with informative articles cannot hope to achieve that end by appearing in little magazines; commercial editors looking for prospective writers of articles do not generally find them by watching the little magazine. And finally, articles and essays of a type not likely to sell to the quality magazines or the slicks are usually sent to non-commercial magazines which specialize in such writing, rather than to the *Prairie Schooner*, which is better known for its fiction and poetry. The writer of a scholarly article, for example, does more for his reputation by publishing it in a scholarly journal than by contributing it to the *Schooner*, and similarly a critic is better off contributing to a critical journal.

Consequently, although it receives stories and poems from all over the United States and from several foreign countries, the *Schooner* does not attract many articles and essays, and Wimberly has frequently been hard pressed to fill the space he wants to devote to those forms. As early as 1932, the *Manuscript Market Guide* listed as the *Schooner*'s most frequent need "good articles and essays, though the magazine is devoted chiefly to fiction." When he does not obtain such contributions through the mail, Wimberly petitions them from faculty members or other local residents. This explains the large proportion of Nebraskans among the contributors of articles and essays.

In an editorial sense, however, the early regionalism of the *Schooner*'s non-fiction prose has, like that of its poetry and fiction, largely given way to a policy of eclecticism.

The term "non-fiction prose" is nearly as broad as it is awkward, and the variety of such prose in the *Schooner* has been as broad as the term—so broad, indeed, that it is difficult to ascertain any editorial principle which has operated in the selection of material. As with fiction and poetry, Wimberly has of course drawn a line against material in bad taste, but in the case of articles or essays this restriction has been largely academic. He has also been prepared to resist making the *Schooner* the special tool of any critical or political group, but as writers know the minor position to which such writing is relegated in the *Schooner*, there has been no concerted drive by any such group to monopolize the space allotted to exposition. In general, then, Wimberly's policy since the break from conscious regionalism has been to select, from the manuscripts available to him, those prose pieces which seem the most interesting and the best written.

If any general preference is visible in Wimberly's selection, it is one for satire. He himself is fond of writing satire and writes it very well, as is demonstrated in most of his *Schooner* articles and in many of his "Ox Cart" comments. One finds there clever but biting attacks on such diverse subjects as Will Rogers, Charles Lindbergh (at a time when he still enjoyed a great popular reputation), Gene Tunney, Republicanism, proletarian writers, American women, Edgar Guest, and modern poetry. There is a touch of irony in Wimberly's comment in the "Ox Cart" for Winter, 1932: "For weal or woe we have again offered space in the *Schooner* to Frederick Laertes Christensen . . . and to Joe Deming. . . . These writers 'can get going' only in case they are out to have fun at the expense of this, or that, or the other thing. But in the *Schooner*, be it said, we permit no writer to indulge himself in indiscriminate satire."

Apart from the rather frequent appearance of satire, the articles and essays in the *Schooner* are characteried only by their variety. They range in style from such rigidly formal academic articles as Robert P. Crawford's "America in Japanese Eyes" (Fall, 1946. "Without assuming to be conclusive, several points deserve comment.") to leisurely personal reminiscences such as August Derleth's "Four Spinsters" (Spring, 1950. "Sometimes, in my nocturnal wandering about in Sac Prairie, I paused here and there, drawn by the old houses. . . ."). In significance, the prose covers an equally broad range. At one end is James Shively's "Willa Cather Juvenilia" (Spring, 1948), which not only discusses a previously ignored phase of the author's life but presents several previously uncollected writings; at the other are such essays as Floyd W. Hoover's "Bullfighting Would Be Cheaper" (Winter, 1947), a satirical commentary on college athletics which is similar in its devices to (and somewhat less successful in its execution than) William McNeil's widely-circulated "race horse" proposal of ten years earlier.[8] Some of the articles are pitched at the level of the specialist in literature and would be at home in such a magazine as the *Sewanee Review*. Outstanding among such pieces are ten penetrating essays by Charles I. Glicksberg, which start with "Symbolism in Proletarian Poetry" (Fall, 1943) and include discussions of "Karl Shapiro and the Per-

---

[8] See Robert M. Hutchins, "Gate Receipts and Glory," *Saturday Evening Post*, December 3, 1938, pp. 23, 73-77.

sonal Accent," "Sartre: Existentialism in Fiction," "The Poetry of Surrealism," and "Shaw the Novelist." Many of the articles, on the other hand, demand no specialized knowledge or interest, and some would fit comfortably into the *Cosmopolitan* or the *Reader's Digest*. In fact five articles first published in the *Schooner* have later appeared in the *Reader's Digest*.[9]

In addition to these miscellaneous contributed pieces, the non-fiction prose of the *Schooner*'s first twenty-five years in-cludes three regular editorial features. One of these, "The Dog in the Manger," ran for two issues in 1929 as a "letters to the editor column," edited by Wilbur Gaffney. After Gaffney's removal to New York it was discontinued until Winter, 1931, when it was revived by William S. Thompson as a vehicle for facetious comment on any convenient subject. The column disappeared with the end of Volume 6 (1932), when space restrictions forced it out.

Of more significance was a book review section which ran through the *Schooner*'s early years. During the first year the feature was titled "Books and Authors" and included reviews written by various residents of Lincoln. With the first issue of 1928, the feature was renamed "Bibliana" and was placed under the complete control of Gilbert H. Doane. Doane, Uni-versity of Nebraska librarian, made the feature an interesting collection of facts and opinions on recent literary publica-tions. When he resigned in 1936, "Bibliana" was retained; each issue contained, under that title, from three to six reviews, often by university faculty members. But in 1938 this section

---

[9] Two of these articles were originally submitted to the *Schooner* and were bought by the *Digest* after their appearance there: Archibald Ed-wards' "Ain't No Deer" (Spring, 1943) and Gerald Kennedy's "Confessions of a Clergyman" (Spring, 1946). The other three were "plants," first accepted by the *Digest*, then directed by that magazine to the *Schooner* for publication before "reprinting": O. K. Armstrong's "He Transformed a Rabble Into an Army" (Winter, 1947), Paul Friggens' "The Bobers of Borzova" (Spring, 1949), and Edwin Muller's "Hybrid Harry" (Winter, 1950).

too was dropped and, except for the four issues of 1940, the *Schooner* did not again carry reviews. Wimberly's comment on the occasion of discontinuing the section points up again the fact that he was more interested in publishing literature than in publishing comments on it:

> The present issue of the *Schooner* omits "Bibliana," our book review section. Whether or not this section will be dropped permanently is a matter now under editorial advisement. One argument in favor of omitting the section is that more space will be available for purely creative or literary writing: stories, poems, and essays, as well as an occasional play. Had "Bibliana" been included in this number it would have meant the exclusion of one of the stories, say, or several of the poems. The question is this: Is it fair to the writer whose story has not yet appeared to make him yield space to a review or notice of a work that has already found its way into print? (Fall, 1938, 230.)

This comment by Wimberly appeared in the "Ox Cart," the longest running and most important of the *Schooner's* editorial features. The "Ox Cart" opened with the magazine's second issue; for its first five appearances it was written by various members of the *Schooner* family, but with the issue for Spring, 1928, Wimberly took over the "Ox Cart," and it has been in his hands ever since.

The "Ox Cart" is valuable for the many indications of policy it contains. It is here that Wimberly has frequently expressed his editorial attitudes as well as his reaction to the world around him. But the feature is equally important for the contributor's notes which it carries. In each issue Wimberly identifies, in the "Ox Cart," each contributor, telling where he lives, giving some biographical information, and indicating his past literary achievements and, if possible, his future literary plans. It is for these notes, rather than for Wimberly's editorial comments, that the "Ox Cart" has been retained when other editorial features were discontinued. For rather than being an imposition on the contributors, these notes are regarded as a service to them. The notes aid the *Schooner* in its function of introducing talented writers to the commercial publishers. Publishers who discover in the *Schooner* work of promise can, by consulting the "Ox Cart," learn more about the author and how to approach him. Although it does occupy space which might be devoted to original contributions, its continuance is consistent with Wimberly's purpose of encouraging the modern American literary artist and furthering his career.

6

Submissions, Rejections and Contributors

ATTEMPTS have sometimes been made to define the "author" as a type. If Wimberly's experience with writers who submit manuscripts to the *Prairie Schooner* is any indication, there is no such type. During its first twenty-five years the *Schooner* received material from an estimated 25,000 people; the heterogeneous nature of this group suggests that the modern writer— or at least the one who submits work to the *Schooner*—is an individual whose only typifying characteristic is the fact that he writes. He may, of course, be man or woman, may be fifteen years old or eighty-five, may have had years of experience or may be testing his talent for the first time. He may devote all of his working hours to writing, or he may be a farmer, lawyer, or hobo, who writes because he likes to or because he feels that he must. He may think himself the most brilliant man of his generation or he may sincerely doubt that he has any ability; and he may be correct in his self-appraisal or he may be dead wrong.

These 25,000 people have become aware of the *Schooner* as a potential market through a variety of means. Some of them, mostly contributors of non-fiction prose, have first submitted work upon Wimberly's invitation. However, unlike some magazines which depend primarily upon solicited items, the *Schooner* usually prints a manuscript not because the editor petitioned it but because the author wanted it printed there. Some of these authors have seen the magazine, bought it, and even subscribed before submitting their work. But the annual number of hopeful contributors far exceeds the total annual circulation of the *Schooner;* most of those submitting have learned of the magazine without ever having seen it. Some of these have been attracted through market guides in such publications as *Writer's Digest,* the *Writer, Manuscript Market Guide, Poetry Digest,* or even the *Oregon Sunday Journal.* Others have seen the name of the *Schooner,* or reprinted selections from it, in the various award annuals, such as the Edward J. O'Brien, O. Henry Memorial, or Thomas Uzzell volumes of short stories, or the Thomas Moult or University of Pennsylvania volumes of poetry.

A surprising number of submissions have come to the *Schooner* through literary agents who are trying to build solid reputations for their clients. Lurton Blassingame, of New York, has sent the work of over a dozen of his clients, including Roderick Lull, Howard McKinley Corning, and Robert Fontaine. Other agents to employ the *Schooner* include Mrs. Michael Amrine, Maxim Lieber, Kenneth MacNichol, Leland Hayward, Inc., and the Central Marketing Service, all of New York, and "The Oldest Writer's Service" of Franklin, Ohio.

But probably the largest group of manuscripts are submitted directly by writers who first learned of the *Schooner* from acquaintances. These writers have submitted at the suggestion of high school teachers of English, college professors, directors of writers' workshops, and editors of other magazines. And, more frequently, they have submitted on the advice of other writers, among them Conrad Aiken, Ralph Cheyney, Jack Conroy, Joseph Joel Keith, Raymond Kresensky, Bernard Raymund, and Byron Herbert Reese.

The individuality of those who, having learned of the *Prairie Schooner*, try to secure publication in its pages extends even to their methods of seeking that publication. Some of them, instead of offering manuscripts for consideration, invite Wimberly to petition their work. Thus a mimeographed post-card reads:

> I am desirous of exchanging articles and short stories for advertising space in your publications.
> Formally I was a Russian Baron an an Officer in the Royal Army. The articles and stories which I will sub-mit to you are of Russia.
> The advertising will be on herbs and cosmetics and will be continous.
> If interested please send me your advertising rates and story prices.
> Awaiting your reply, I am
> Sincerily Yours;
>
> (December, 1932)[1]

And a letter carries this offer:

> Please let me know whether or not you pay for short stories, and if so how much you pay.
> My stories cover one sheet of typewritten matter. Some take two to six full sheets the size of this sheet. I would send several stories to you for inspection if you wish.
> I can write two or more sheets daily; that is, ready for the press. Each story would fill an average page of a book; therefore, about three hundred fifty would be sufficient for a book. I think it is possible for me to write enough for two books yearly, especially by utilizing the Dictaphones—I have a complete outfit of dictating machines, also two typewriters.
> Is it possible to join you in your work? (June, 1933)

---

[1] Correspondence reprinted here is in the posession of Dr. Wimberly. Originals have been followed in all details, including spelling and punctuation. Some signatures have, for obvious reasons, been withheld.

Most of those who seek to publish in the *Schooner,* however, follow the practice which Wimberly prefers, that of submitting their manuscripts without any preliminary communication. Usually the manuscripts carry covering letters from their authors. These letters furnish considerable insight into the variety of writers who submit to the *Schooner.*

Sometimes the letter is brief and considerate: "When there is a breathing spell during these hot days will you sometime read this story?—Thanks!" Sometimes it is brief but less considerate: "I'm enclosing a new story. I hope you like it. Please let me know your decision in a week."

Occasionally the would-be contributor tries to impress with his cleverness:

> I here submit
> Nine metric skits,
> For your attention and appraisel.
> Dear Editor
> If you want more,
> Show me your journal pays well. (March, 1935)

Or he may try to appeal to Wimberly's sympathies:

> Now, Mr. Wimberly, I hate to put a sob story as badly as the next one but I've been working hard at this writing game for a number of years and I've yet to make my first scratch. This letter is to inquire, in fact, plead, that if you consider my story worthy of publication in the Prairie Schooner you will hold it until you can use it. Before I get so old I won't be able to pound a typewriter, I should like to see some of my work in print in a worthwhile magazine. Will you do this for me? Someday maybe I can repay the favor. (November, 1932)

Or again, he may try to purchase acceptance, as in the case of an Arkansas woman who offered Wimberly a goose-feather pillow if he would print her poem.

Some of those submitting try to secure Wimberly's acceptance while saving him the trouble of reading the manuscript:

> I am attaching a short story . . . which you may find suitable to your needs in a future issue. You may not care for the title. . . . At any rate, I hope you print the story. It is good. Predominantly a character study, it does not avoid narrative material. There is originality in the idea and in the treatment of it. Warm humanity and utter lack of surface sophistication increase its appeal. (August, 1933).

And some of them unintentionally save him that trouble:

> I am mailing one of my poems Intitled Just a Roamer in which I just finished writing. I more poems Inwchich I will mail in later. If you are interested in em. The Name of those are Mother dear, and Gossip. Hoping to hear from you soon. (May, 1954)

Accompanying letters, however, whether good or bad, have little if any effect on the final disposition of a manuscript. Wimberly prefers that any such letter present objective facts about the submitter—not to help in the editorial decision, but to provide material for the "Ox Cart" in case of acceptance. The manuscript itself should preferably be typed, double-spaced, with adequate margins for editorial comment and correction. The author's name and full address should appear on the first page of the manuscript and on the enclosed return envelope. Wimberly prefers that return postage be enclosed loose, so that in case of the manuscript's acceptance the postage can be returned. Occasionally, rejected manuscripts cannot be returned because the submitter has forgotten to give his name or address. More frequently the writer fails to include return postage; in the rare case that failure is intentional: "If not acceptable, I'll send return postage." (August, 1934)

Such uninformed practices are, however, in the minority. Most of those who send manuscripts to the *Schooner,* the experienced writers and the thoughtful ones, make their submissions in a manner which, if it does not follow the letter of Wimberly's prescription, at least does not unduly complicate his job as editor.

In the *Schooner*'s infancy Wimberly gave his personal attention to every manuscript received. It was not difficult for him to do so. In fact, in its early days as a campus magazine the *Schooner* was so hard-pressed for contributors that pseudonyms were sometimes employed to disguise the deficiency. Thus, in addition to using his own name, Loren Eiseley published poems as "Eronel Croye," "Silas Amon," and "Tlo Honda," while poems by Wilbur Gaffney are credited to "Elizabeth Brander" and "M. R. Lowe." But as the *Schooner*'s reputation spread, the problem of securing contributions was replaced by that of giving adequate attention to all manuscripts received. By 1935 the *Schooner* was receiving from 1,500 to 2,000 manuscripts annually and publishing about one in twenty (Spring, 1935, 154). Ten years later it was receiving 2,500 a year and publishing about one in thirty (Fall, 1945, 263). It was physically impossible for Wimberly, with his double duties as teacher[2] and editor, to give his personal attention to all contributions received. He began to enlist aid in the first reading of the manuscripts. For the most part this aid has come from Frederick L. Christensen, who has been associate editor of the magazine since 1928.

Christensen was born in central Nebraska, in 1903. Except for ten years in Wyoming as a boy, he has lived in Nebraska ever since. He entered the University of Nebraska in 1925, and became an honor student. Although not a charter member, he joined the local chapter of Sigma Upsilon shortly after it

[2] Wimberly, who has been a full professor since 1929, carries a full academic load of four classes each semester. He normally conducts a sophomore survey of literature, an advanced course in seventeenth-century literature, and two courses in creative writing. He is also one of the most popular advisors of candidates for advanced degrees in English.

was founded. With the first issue of the second volume, he joined the staff of the *Schooner,* where he worked largely as a proofreader while completing work toward his bachelor's degree (1928) and his master's (1929). In 1929 he joined the English department as an assistant to Dr. Wimberly, and at the same time he assumed a more responsible role in the editing of the *Schooner.* In the "Ox Cart" for Summer, 1938, Wimberly wrote: "Frederick L. Christensen, assistant in English, is one of the chief editorial props of the *Schooner.* God only knows what the magazine would do without him." Christensen has done some ghost writing but has published nothing of significance outside the *Schooner.* His editorial experience includes two years (April, 1940, to March, 1942) as editor of the *Nebraska Scholar,* "A Review of Current Research and Scholarship at the University of Nebraska."

Since early in the 1930's, a manuscript addressed to the *Schooner* has ordinarily passed first through the hands of Christensen. It is his function to weed out and return those many manuscripts which are obviously unacceptable to the *Schooner* and to pass on to Wimberly those which show any potentiality. Through long association with Wimberly, both as associate editor of the *Schooner* and as a reader for Wimberly's composition courses at the university, Christensen has become closely familiar with Wimberly's standards and tastes; but he is careful to make all questionable decisions in the author's favor, never returning a manuscript holding the slightest promise without first obtaining Wimberly's opinion. Some few submissions—those from writers whose work in the past has consistently merited careful consideration—he turns over to Wimberly immediately, without a preliminary reading.

On the average about three-fourths of the manuscripts received by the *Schooner* are returned by Christensen; the other fourth reach Wimberly's desk, where they are carefully considered in the light of those standards discussed in the preceding chapter.

A manuscript which clears the first hurdle and receives Wimberly's consideration may experience a variety of fates. It may find no favor and be returned immediately, with a brief penned note expressing thanks for the submission. (The *Schooner* has no printed rejection slip.) Or it may be accepted intact, for publication in the next issue. But most manuscripts experience a reception between those two extremes. It is in his handling of these other manuscripts that Wimberly works hardest and performs his most important and valuable editorial services.

Many manuscripts which Wimberly receives are rejected because of some basic weakness in their conception or some serious organic flaw in their construction—a triteness of theme, for example, or an excessive ingenuity of plot. But sometimes Wimberly can discern through the unacceptable piece of work flashes of promise in its author—a freshness of style or tone, or a competence in the handling of individual details and situations. If Wimberly thinks he sees some such promise, however slight, he returns the manuscript with an encouraging note, always inviting the writer to submit further evidence of his work and usually pointing out the specific weakness which made the rejected manuscript unacceptable.

Once in a great while such rejection offends the writer. One Denver poet wrote, when her first submission to the *Schooner* was returned with Wimberly's note of rejection:

> I am amazed! I thought that poem especially suited to The Prairie Schooner—born for it. I thought I was being especially thoughtful in offering it to you. It delighted me to have something so appropriate. I cannot help feeling astonished at your reception of it. I am afraid I would fear to send you anything more. I would not dare to trust my own judgment on what would please you. (March, 1933)

An even more violent reaction was expressed by a woman from the state of Washington, after her poem was rejected:

I have received your letter (interesting work) and my poem. . . . I read my fine poem once again, looked at your handsome letter head and wondered. Why do you call it Prairie Schooner? Better name it Feathery Dawn, Blown Leaves, or Fraid Of The Light, something of that sort. I have never seen a copy of it I admit, but I will wager you did not publish a line in the last year that was remembered two hours after it was read.

If you are afraid to publish ballads about American life why call your magazine Prairie Schooner? The prairie schooner means nothing to anybody any where except in America.

Why do you advise me to send it to Household Magazine? The poem is not about cooking or embroidery or the care of children. I know why you did it. It was because you felt guilty in rejecting it. You should feel guilty. Editors of poetry magazines are doing nothing for American poetry. You encourage only those who "dabble in pastel shades of subtle emotion." You are shy, timid and self conscious. You are ashamed rather than proud of your heritage, rich as it is. You publish no vital poetry. Not because it is not being written. Because the poet who has something to say cannot get a hearing. Your magazines are read only by scared little lady poets and a few tired grammarians. If you really wanted to make Americans love poetry again you would publish verse that would move the common people.

I dare you to contradict me. (February, 1937)

Fortunately for Wimberly's disposition, such letters arrive but seldom. An overwhelming majority of those writers in whom Wimberly shows any interest are appreciative of his comments and inspired by his encouragement:

Yours has been the kindest note I have ever received in my short career as a sender of poems and a receiver of slips. (March, 1936)

Your kind note of criticism . . . is deeply appreciated. I wish all editors were human. A kind word or two eases so much the weary journey of one who is determined to arrive. (March, 1935)

If you could know what it means to acknowledge your-self a failure and see nothing ahead of you as I did today —and then to get your two letters, perhaps you could understand how grateful I am to you. It was like giving me back life. All the hardship under which I'm writing somehow seems to be compensated by the encourage-ment you have given me. (December, 1932)

Your generous note came in the nick o' time. Thank you—from my innermost depths—for saving me from complete despair. I had quite decided that if you re-fused [my story], I'd never try to write another line of fiction. . . . Now I'm working like mad on "the so-called realistic type of story." (September, 1932)

Most of the writers thus encouraged to continue writing submit further efforts to the *Schooner*.

You have been so generous with personal criticism and help on two previous manuscripts that I dare to send this, hoping that it may make the Schooner, or, if not, that I may at least have your opinion of it. (July, 1931)

Last month I sent to you two stories which I had hoped would be worthy of publication in your magazine. You returned them to me with a very kindly note asking, "Have you others?" Your personal message was the most encouraging influence turned my way since I first began to hope for seeing my work in print. I am en-closing another attempt at the quality of writing that you desire. (November, 1932)

With persistent effort I may soon find something worthy of publication in Prairie Schooner. I appreciate your telling me why my former attempts were not acceptable, and I shall try to conform to your needs. (December, 1932)

Many thanks for your criticism of my story . . . which I recently submitted to your magazine. Let me say that it is the first real help or encouragement I have received in the several years during which I have been trying to make the first rung of the ladder. . . . Believe me that such encouragement and pointed criticism as your letter contains make the path less vague and brighten the prospect of continued striving. Please, then, don't think my sending this other manuscript to be a presumption upon the kindness your letter evinces, but remember that such advice is invaluable to a person in my position. (July, 1931)

By encouraging and obtaining such further submissions, Wimberly of course greatly increases his duties as editor; he spends extra time not only in writing the personal rejections but also in reading the additional manuscripts which they invite. Often his efforts are a waste of his own time and of the prospective contributor's; the suspected talent proves to have been an illusion or, instead of maturing, it weakens and dies. But many of the writers thus encouraged eventually produce something which Wimberly is happy to publish. Carl Uhlarik sent in at least a dozen stories and sketches before he finally appeared in the *Schooner* with his story "The Bittersweet Next Year" (Winter, 1937). George Snell submitted periodically for ten years before placing his story "The Pilgrimage" (Fall, 1943). Clarence Alva Powell achieved his first success with the *Schooner* after more than twelve years of submitting, and Hannah Kahn after about five. Indeed, few of the contributors to the *Schooner* were successful on their first attempt. Had Wimberly been unable to elicit further submissions from those whom he at first rejected, little that makes up the contents of the *Schooner*'s first twenty-five volumes would have been available to him.

In addition to those submissions which are organically weak but demonstrate some talent, Wimberly receives many manuscripts which are basically good but contain remediable defects which bar their acceptance. Thus a short story may have a weak conclusion or lack a sufficient motivating incident, while a poem may contain an inconsistency of imagery or a few dissonant lines. When Wimberly finds a manuscript which is unacceptable in its present form but which might be salvaged by revision, his letter of rejection carries advice to that effect. Almost without exception such advice results in a resubmission of the manuscript, sometimes a year or more after the first submission, but more often within a week or two. Writers occasionally register a mild protest against the suggested changes, even after they have been accomplished. But in the majority of cases they appear not only willing but eager to make the changes, which they accept as improvements.[3] Thus Melville Cane wrote on May 16, 1944:

> Thank you for your letter of the 13th suggesting a less brutal ending to my story "Mr. Samuels." I approve of the suggestion and have attempted to adopt it, as you will see by the enclosed new ending. Let me know if you think this does the trick. It is unusually kind of you to be ready to criticize constructively. Certainly, it is not common with the editors I have encountered.

Cane's reaction to Wimberly's criticism has been duplicated, in only slightly different words, by literally scores of writers to whom Wimberly has returned manuscripts. Here, for example, are the comments of four writers who subsequently became *Schooner* contributors:

> Mark Schorer: Thank you so very much for letter anent my story "Minna Is Left Alone." I have revised the tale in accordance with your suggestions and am returning it to you herewith. . . . I am truly grateful for your suggestions since I do feel that the story is almost tangibly strengthened. (January, 1933)

> Weldon Kees: Thanks very much for your letter and comments on "Saturday Rain." I've lengthened it according to your suggestions, and I think it's much improved. I appreciated your interest a great deal, and

---

[3] It has been Wimberly's experience that the writer who has already "arrived" is much more receptive to suggestions, and more likely to follow them, than the novice.

hope that perhaps you may be able to use this ms. now. (May, 1934)

Ralph Friedrich: Thank you very much for your letter concerning "Record of a Dream." I have altered it in accordance with your suggestions, and I am submitting it again. Let me say that I value your criticism and that, if you think the story still unsatisfactory, I shall be willing to make other alterations. (March, 1935)

David Bernstein: I am sending you the revised version of my story, "The Wool," which I have worked on according to your suggestions. . . . Your letter of criticism encouraged me greatly, and I want to thank you for it. I think that, in following it, I've made a much better story out of "The Wool," and I'd rather see it in Prairie Schooner than in any other magazine I can think of. Again, thank you. (May, 1935)

All four of those men revised their manuscripts to Wimberly's satisfaction; in each case the contribution marked the writer's first appearance in the *Schooner,* and in three of the cases it was the writer's first published story. It seems clear that Wimberly's method of dealing with the unaccepted but revisable manuscript is profitable both to the *Schooner* and to the writer who receives the editorial suggestions.

Some of the manuscripts received by the *Schooner* are on the whole acceptable for publication but contain flaws which, while not necessitating return of the manuscript, do require attention. Purely mechanical errors, such as obvious mistakes in spelling, punctuation, grammar, or syntax, Wimberly sometimes corrects without consulting the author. If, however, the emendations involve any matters of taste or judgment, Wimberly writes a letter tentatively accepting the manuscript but requesting permission to make the proposed changes.

The proposed changes may be of a minor sort: the substitution of one word for another, the use of a more attractive title, or the simplification of a complicated sentence structure. While easily effected, they may be more serious in their nature:

the omission of a stanza, a paragraph, or a page, or the re-ordering of elements in the manuscript. Or the changes may involve Wimberly's rewriting a passage or giving detailed recommendations for such rewriting.

Popular tradition portrays the author as a sensitive but confident person who, unless he be dishonest, would rather starve unpublished than let the editor (who is tradionally stupid and unliterary) ruin his stuff by changing a single word. The writers whom Wimberly has encountered do not fit into that popular conception; very rarely does one of them balk at making or accepting a suggested change. One little-known poet, when asked to change the title of his poem and to omit a quotation in Greek which appeared as a motto over the poem, assumed the stereotyped attitude with an elaborate defense:

> I'm afraid the . . . title will have to stand; after all it says what the verse is, and that, I suspect, is the first business of a title.
>
> As to the Greek quotation, I don't want to be too insistent. Still, I should like to keep it. *One*: it won't make any difference to those who can't read it, and a single line of type won't get in their way. To those that can read it, (*two*) it's my source and an acknowledge-ment that ought in all honesty to be made, and (*three*) it contains, at least by implication, an idea which I think is important for a good deal of verse and prose, and (*four*) it sort of throws down an essential challenge in this whole business of originality and novelty in crea-tive work. . . . Now that I've made my plea, if you still think the Greek doesn't justify the space it's going to take to print it, I regretfully give permission for its deletion. (August, 1938)

In this case Wimberly had to take what he could get, keep-ing the title and omitting the epigraph. His objection to the Greek had nothing to do with space. It was dictated partially by his conviction that the motto was overly esoteric and that it would "make a difference" to those who couldn't read it, but primarily by his knowledge that the press had no suitable font of Greek type.

But, whether from conviction or ambition, nearly all of the *Schooner* contributors show an apparently genuine willingness to make or permit suggested alterations, and most of them appear grateful for Wimberly's corrections:

> Copies of the Schooner reached me some days back. My story, with the few wise intrusions of your blue pencil, appears to advantage. I'm glad you touched it up. (February, 1933)

> The suggested revision of page 4 . . . is fine and improves the story very much. Many thanks. (August, 1941)

> Read your letter and really agree that the ending on page 6 is a "beaut"—I realized it at once. (March, 1944)

> As you will see, I have accepted all your changes; I find them very appropriate and an improvement on the original. (August, 1944)

The extent to which some contributors trust Wimberly's editorial judgment and literary ability is indicated by the manner in which they give him complete authority to decide on the final form of their work:

> I shall be glad to have you make any deletions in my poem . . . which you consider advisable. (January, 1943)

> It is all right with me if you want to edit or cut down [my story] any way you see fit. I'm glad you're using it. (August, 1943)

> If there is any question about the position of paragraphs, I leave it to your judgment. (January, 1945)

> *Please* do not hestitate to change words, sentences, titles, anything which in your opinion will improve my

work. If you did not know better than I, *you* would be
the struggling tyro, not the Editor as you are. (October,
1947)

On the whole, as the foregoing letters indicate, Wimberly's
relationship with those who submit to the *Schooner* has been
amicable and characterized by mutual respect. Occasionally
this relationship has been marred by irritation over the handling of manuscripts. The author's complaint is that Wimberly
holds the manuscript too long; Wimberly's that the author demands the manuscript too soon.

The most annoying letter that Wimberly receives is the one
requesting return of a manuscript because it has been accepted
by another market. The practice of sending one piece of work
to several magazines and waiting for the earliest acceptance is
viewed by Wimberly as an unpardonable sin, and he begrudges
every second spent on handling a manuscript which must be
returned for that reason. One writer submitted a manuscript
on November 29, 1947, and recalled it on December 1 for
publication elsewhere. But fortunately for Wimberly's state
of mind, such occurrences are rare.

More frequent, and only slightly less annoying, is the inquiry as to the disposition of a manuscript which Wimberly
has not had time to consider. In market indexes, the *Schooner*
is listed as reporting "in a month," which is about average for
the little magazines. Wimberly tries to stay within that limit,
but he appreciates a few days of grace; and it antagonizes him
to be asked, two or three weeks after a manuscript has been
received, to write an assurance that it has not been lost.

Sometimes, however, the author's inquiry is justified.
Though he tries to guard against it, Wimberly occasionally
delays his final decision until considerably more than a month
has passed. He has never lost a submission, but he has given
writers grounds for worry or annoyance. This happened with
some frequency during the depression '30's, when Wimberly
could never be sure that another issue of the *Schooner* would

appear or, if it did, how many pages it would contain. Several writers complained, with considerable restraint and understanding, about going two or three months without any report. And at least one felt compelled to use a threatening tone:

> Several months ago I sent you a short story which has not been returned, nor have I had reply regarding it. Certainly you received the manuscript, because the envelope carried my return address. A card which I wrote you regarding the matter has been ignored. Unless you return the manuscript or in some way assure me of its safe-keeping, I shall take steps with my attorney to recover this property, or the value thereof. . . . Although the thing may be worthless to you, I hold it to be of somewhat higher value.

Later in the *Schooner*'s career, this time during the crisis of the war years, there came a small rash of complaints on another score. Several poets who had received notices of acceptance waited through issue after issue for their poems to appear. Thus Mykia Taylor's "Even Your Mirth" waited two years for publication, LeGarde Doughty's "Passage in Library" waited three years, and Mary Willis Shelburne's "Found in an Ancient Place" waited three and a half. The explanation is simple enough. Wimberly had inadvertently accepted too many poems. And, as the *Schooner* publishes only every three months, it took some time to work through the backlog.

But these cases, like the letters from submitters impatient for a report, are exceptions in the *Schooner*'s routine and, when set over the total number of submissions, constitute an almost infinitesimal fraction. Most manuscripts received by Wimberly are reported on within three or four weeks.[4] And

---

[4] It is interesting to compare Wimberly's practice with reports received on short stories sent to eight magazines over the period July 15, 1953 to January 11, 1954. One story was submitted to each magazine. Following is the length of time it took each to report; in parentheses are the announced

the writer whose manuscript is accepted almost always becomes a "contributor" with the appearance of the next issue
of the *Schooner*.

Of the estimated 25,000 hopeful contributors to the *Schooner* during its first twenty-five years, 1,080 have, through Wimberly's acceptance, become actual contributors. Of that number, 510 first appeared as poets, 320 as the authors of fiction,
and 247 as the authors of essays or articles. Many of them
have appeared only once in the *Schooner;* on the other hand,
August Derleth's name appeared over seventeen contributions
during the *Schooner*'s first twenty-five years, Rudolph Umland's over twenty-four, Harold Vinal's over twenty-eight, and
Loren Eiseley's over thirty-seven. Some of the contributors
have never appeared elsewhere in print, but most of them
have published in at least a few other magazines, and many
of them have written prolifically.[5]

Over thirty per cent of the contributors have been residents
of Nebraska at the time of first submitting, and states in prox-
imity to Nebraska (Illinois, Iowa, Missouri, Colorado, Kansas,
Oklahoma, Wyoming, and South Dakota) are also generously
represented in the list. Obviously the *Schooner* has fulfilled
its original purpose of providing a literary outlet for Nebraska
and midwestern writers. The rest of the list, however, indicates the extent to which the *Schooner* has outgrown its orig-

times, as listed in *The Writer's Market: Accent*, 32 days (three weeks);
Hudson Review, 23 days (one month); *Partisan Review*, 56 days (several
weeks); *Sewanee Review*, 46 days (no promise); *Story*, 83 days (no promise);
Virginia Quarterly Review, 114 days (two weeks); *Western Review*, 42 days
(one month) *Yale Review*, 52 days (three weeks). Only two of the magazines, *Accent* and the *Virginia Quarterly Review*, sent personal notes of
rejection. The other six used printed rejection slips.

[5] Derleth, for example, has been a prodigious writer; by the end of
1946 he had written some fifty published books and edited a dozen more,
in addition to contributing to nearly 250 magazines and metropolitan
newspapers. And he is still very active.

inal boundaries. Included among the contributors are writers from all of the forty-eight states except Idaho and New Hampshire. Also represented are Arabia, Argentina, Canada, Cuba, the Dominican Republic, England, Hawaii, India, Ireland, Italy, Mexico, the Philippines, Scotland, and Sweden. New York and California, with 126 and 114 contributors respectively, have each produced more *Schooner* contributors than any other state except Nebraska; among contributors of either of the two more strictly literary forms, poetry and fiction, the combined totals from these two states exceed the number from Nebraska.

A common method of appraising a magazine's contributor list (and by extension, evaluating the magazine itself) is by noting its "discoveries"—by which is meant the writers whom the magazine has been the first to publish.[6] If one counts the "firsts" carried by the *Schooner* during its first twenty-five years, he finds a total of nearly three hundred, most of them Nebraskans and many of them students at the university.

It is difficult, in the case of a magazine still appearing, to estimate the combined value of the writers it has introduced. Except in the rare case, there is a lapse of time between the author's first promise and his ultimate fulfillment. Sometimes that lapse is considerable. Nebraska's Bess Furman, for example, while working as a reporter on the Omaha *World-Herald,* was introduced by the *Schooner* with a rollicking bit of humor, "Heart Throbs Bona Fide" (Spring, 1929). She then went to Washington, D. C., and worked as a journalist until 1949, when her autobiographical *Washington By-line* thrust her name into the current literary scene. A second book in 1951, *White House Profile,* was more widely reviewed and was received with such unanimity of praise that the

---

[6] One customarily ignores earlier publication in such media as small newspapers, high school annuals, college fun-sheets, or anything not copyrighted, and any reportorial writing.

Schooner could now refer with pride to its "discovery" of Mrs. Furman.

A similar case is that of another Nebraskan, Marion Edward Stanley. Stanley, as a student member of the group which founded the *Schooner,* helped "discover" himself with two poems in Volume I, Number 1. After leaving the University of Nebraska he worked for nearly twenty years as a journalist, first with the Associated Press, then with the Office of War Information, and finally as executive editor of *Coronet* and *Esquire* magazines. Then, during an illness, he decided to resign from the business side of literature and devote himself to writing.[7] The reception accorded his first two historical novels, *Thomas Forty* (1947) and *The Rock Cried Out* (1949), more than justified his decision and at the same time added significance to another *Schooner* find.

It is dangerous, then, to pronounce final judgment on the achievement of any *Schooner* contributor so long as he is alive. However, the record to date, coupled with the mathematical odds against literary success, suggests that by far the majority of the *Schooner*'s discoveries are of little long-range significance, having flashed across the pages of the *Schooner* on their way from oblivion to oblivion. They are people who had one or two tales to tell or poems to recite and who happened to place them with Wimberly. Some of those isolated contributions are so good that it is difficult to believe their authors will not be heard from further. Such, for example, is Robert Hutchinson's "Lovely Free Gift" (Winter, 1946), which won the $100 first prize in a Thomas Y. Crowell short story contest. On the record, however, Hutchinson has failed thus far to fulfill the promise of that first story.

The *Schooner* does not number among its discoveries any writers whose current reputations place them in the very front rank of American authors. There are no Eliots, Hemingways,

[7] Letter, July 11, 1949.

or Faulkners in the list. There are several, however, whose achievements since their first printing are sufficient to make Wimberly happy for having given them their start.

Some of these successful discoveries are Nebraskans. The first issue introduced, in addition to Mari Sandoz and Edward Stanley, Martin Severin Peterson, who contributed to the *Schooner* regularly over the next eighteen years. Peterson's special talent, as displayed in the *Schooner,* was the writing of informative prose; he later used that talent in his three published biographies, the best known of which is his entertaining though scholarly *Joaquin Miller, Literary Frontiersman* (1937). In the July issue for 1927, the *Schooner* carried the first of its eight poems by another talented Nebraska writer, Helene Magaret. Miss Magaret's first published long narrative poem, *The Great Horse* (1937) brought her high praise in the pages of *Poetry* magazine, the *Saturday Review of Literature,* and the New York *Times;* but even more important in establishing her reputation were such historical novels as *Father DeSmet* (1940) and *Gailhac of Béziers* (1946). Dorothy Thomas, whose poetry had already appeared in the issues of Winter and Spring of 1928, published her first short story, "The Beast Room," in the issue for Fall of that year. Subsequently she contributed many short stories to the commercial magazines, and she has written two successful novels, *Ma Jeeter's Girls* (1933) and *The Home Place* (1936). Another Nebraska novelist was introduced with the Summer issue of 1932—Virginia Faulkner, who was to delight many of her contemporaries with her gay, sophisticated, and somewhat naughty society novels: *Friends and Romans* (1934), *The Barbarians* (1935) and *My Hey-day; or, The Crack-up of the International Set* (1940).

One of the most versatile Nebraskans to be introduced through the pages of the *Schooner* is painter-author Weldon Kees, who was first printed in the Fall issue for 1934. His name has since appeared frequently in the Edward J. O'Brien-Martha

Foley short story listings. His poetry has been published in many of the little magazines, in several anthologies, and in three collected volumes, *The Last Man* (1943), *The Fall of the Magicians* (1947), and *Poems 1947-1954*. He is also known for his penetrating critical articles and reviews. And Mr. Kees is still a young man, the major portion of whose career should lie in the future.

Other Nebraskans who are today known to many and who were introduced through the *Schooner* include Loren C. Eiseley, who has published a great deal of both poetry and prose in the little and "quality" magazines; Chalmer O. Richardson, author of the novel *The Golden Empire* (1938) and the autobiographical volume *A School in the Country* (1940); and, of course, Lowry C. Wimberly.

The *Schooner* has, then, introduced several competent Nebraska writers. Some of its more noteworthy finds, however, have come from places far distant from Nebraska. Among them are Jesse Stuart from Kentucky, Warren Beck from Wisconsin, and Jessamyn West from California.

Jesse Stuart's introduction came in the issue for Fall, 1930, with a poem "Desolation." During the next twenty years Stuart published about 1,400 poems and 400 stories.[8] Among the anthologies in which his work has appeared are seven consecutive issues of the O'Brien-Foley short-story annual (1937 through 1943). His seventeen books published through 1954 include his Book-of-the-Month-Club selection *Taps for Private Tussie* (1943); his well-received first volume of poetry, *Man with a Bull-tongue Plow* (1934); such short story collections as *Head o' W-Hollow* (1936), *Men of the Mountains* (1941), and *Clearing in the Sky* (1950); and his two personal narratives, *Beyond Dark Hills* (1938) and *The Thread that Runs So True* (1949).

Warren Beck's first published story was "Shadow of a Green Olive Tree" (Spring, 1937). That deftly handled story of

[8] Letter, October 23, 1950.

a young boy's emotions represented an auspicious debut; it was subsequently reprinted in three anthologies and was, in the opinion of many critics, the most effective story in Beck's first collection, *The Blue Sash* (1941). His subsequent publications include a large number of stories, five of which have been reprinted in the O'Brien-Foley annuals; two more volumes of stories, *The First Fish* (1947) and *The Far Whistle* (1951); and three novels, *Final Score* (1944), *Pause Under the Sky* (1947), and *Into Thin Air* (1951).

In the issue for Summer of 1940 the *Schooner* carried a warmly humorous Quaker story, "Music on the Muscatatuck," by Jessamyn West. Miss West firmly established her reputation five years later with her first volume of short stories, *The Friendly Persuasion* (1945). She added to that reputation with her opera *A Mirror for the Sky* (1948) and her novels *The Witch Diggers* (1951) and *Cress Delahanty* (1954). During her relatively short career she has published stories in most of the better American markets, has had four of them reprinted in the O'Brien-Foley annuals, and has had several more (including "Music on the Musatatuck") included in other anthologies.

The list of writers who have gone on to bigger markets after their introduction through the *Schooner* could be further extended. In 1939 the *Schooner* carried the first published story by Leon Surmelian; that story, "I Ask You, Ladies and Gentlemen" (Summer, 1939), gave the title to Surelian's much applauded first book, which appeared in 1945. And the *Schooner* has carried the first published stories of George Albee from California, Ralph Friedrich from Ohio, and Roderick Lull from Oregon. There are, in addition, several younger finds whose reputations have yet to be established but who, judging from their early work, seem destined to achieve some success. Among these are the fiction writers Hoke Norris, Bill Ornstein, Charles Tekeyan, and Emilie Glen, and the Nebraska poet Bernice Slote, whose poems already published would, if collected, constitute a major achievement.

Wimberly takes a realistic view of his role as "discoverer." Concerning the notable "discovery" which opened the *Schooner*'s first issue, he wrote (Spring, 1936, 92) : "We are modest, to the point, at least, of suspecting that Miss Sandoz would have been discovered anyhow."

There is much to commend in Wimberly's admission. The cataloguing of writers introduced by a magazine is a pleasant game, and impressive results may serve as a sort of non-negotiable compensation to otherwise unpaid or underpaid editors. Such results may even be a tentative indication of a magazine's value. But too much is often made of a magazine's "discoveries." The beginning writer normally submits his work to any magazine which he thinks might publish it. And the editor's perspicacity or the quality of his magazine may have less to do with determining who makes the "discovery" than such considerations as publication dates, available space, previous commitments, and of course the uneven qualities of some writers' early works.

The very word "discover" is misleading as a synonym for "publish first." Editors can seldom be said to "discover" a writer in the normal sense of the word, unless they can properly be said to discover their morning mail. The word is more accurately, and significantly, applied in its older sense of "to make known." Little magazines as a group may legitimately take great credit for having brought to the attention of critics and commercial publishers most of America's foremost modern writers. The discovery in this second sense of the word may occasionally—in the case of very talented writers and very lucky ones—be accomplished with the author's first or second appearance in print. But more often he is discovered only through several appearances, and several magazines have a part in making him known. More significant than the question of a magazine's "firsts," therefore, is the question of its general willingness to publish unknown writers of merit and thus assist in their true discovery.

Of the 1,080 contributors to the first twenty-five volumes of the *Schooner,* about 300 had never before been published, and most of the rest had appeared only a few times, in magazines of small circulation. According to the listings in the Library of Congress catalogue, only 174 had published a book prior to their appearance in the *Schooner.* That the *Schooner* generally boosts writers on their way up is indicated by the over-all record of its contributors. The same catalogue, with supplements through 1951, lists over 1,300 books by 367 *Schooner* contributors.[9] And of course many of those who contributed through 1951 have not yet reached the peak of their production.

The *Schooner* has, through early publication, furthered the careers of many writers high in the current literary scale. It published Eudora Welty within a year of her first appearance in the short-lived *Manuscript* (Athens, Ohio), and over the years 1937 and 1938 the *Schooner* carried three of the fourteen stories which made up Miss Welty's first published volume, *A Curtain of Green* (1941). It was one of the first magazines to carry Albert Halper, printing him in 1931, two years before his first appearance in an anthology or his first novel, *Union Square.* Truman Capote appeared in the *Schooner* in 1945, when he was 21; this was before he had been anthologized and three years before his first published book, *Other Voices, Other Rooms.* Richard Sullivan's second magazine appearance was in the *Schooner,* as were Ira Jan Wallach's and Hal Ellson's. Norman Macleod appeared there when he was only 23, five years before his first collection of poems was published. William March launched his highly successful writing career in 1930 with two stories, published almost simultaneously by the *Midland* and the *Prairie Schooner.* Among others whose early careers were furthered by publication in the *Schooner* are Mary Deasy, David Cornel DeJong, Mark Schorer, the prolific August Derleth, Lenard Kaufman, and Robert Tallant. Poets in the group include George Abbe, Byron Herbert Reece, Harry Roskolenko, Winfield Townley Scott, Alan Swallow, and José Garcia Villa.

The *Schooner* has, then, helped a great many beginning writers, either by giving them their first publication or by printing their work early in their careers, when they were struggling to build a reputation. But there have also been— and these are among Wimberly's more painful memories—the opportunities missed. Benjamin Appel is a case in point. The *Schooner* carried an article by Appel in 1931, the same year in which his fiction was discovered by the *Midland;* but, although Appel submitted at least six short stories to the *Schooner* during the years 1931 to 1933, not one of them was accepted for publication. Peter DeVries submitted several times during the early 1930's, with the same lack of success. And Wimberly will probably never forget the morning on which he slipped the strange "experimental" Armenian sketch into its return envelope and sent it back to its unknown author, William Saroyan.

Such rejections are unfortunate for the editor; they lead to later bad publicity or, at best, they sacrifice a future opportunity for good publicity. But they are inescapable risks of the editor's profession. Sometimes the rejected early manuscript is not up to the general level of the work which makes the author's subsequent reputation. But even if the story is a good one, and the editor recognizes that fact, there is a possibility that it may find its way home unpublished. It is a matter of mathematics. And it demonstrates the need for more good magazines, rather than the critical debility of the offending editor.

With twenty or thirty manuscripts competing for space which will accommodate only one, Wimberly often finds that good, publishable stories must be returned. Take again, for example, the case of Benjamin Appel, and assume that the early stories he submitted were as good as those which he has published elsewhere. During the three years in which he was actively trying to break into the *Schooner* with his fiction (years in which the depression restricted the magazine's size), the *Schooner* carried forty-three stories by forty-two authors. Of those forty-three stories, all but three were starred in the O'Brien yearbook, giving the *Schooner* the extremely high rating of 93 per cent over that three-year period. More than half of the stories received two stars or more, and twelve stories of the forty-three, or 28 per cent, received the three stars which constitute the annual's highest praise. Among the forty-three stories are the first *Schooner* appearances of George Albee and Albert Halper, Raymond Kresensky and José Garcia Villa, David Cornel DeJong and Mark Schorer. Others against whom Appel was competing include Emmett Gowen, Howard McKinley Corning, Earl Cranston Ewert, Solon R. Barber, Upton Terrell, Grace Stone Coates, and Mary K. Rhodes.

Wimberly might, when faced with the necessity of excluding good publishable manuscripts, retain them for a later number; but that would only increase the problem of making selections for the next issue, and the practice, if continued, would eventually lead to a closetful of excellent unpublished material belonging to irate unpublished authors.

Or again, to avoid accidentally rejecting authors whom he might later be proud to claim, he might print all the available "firsts" or "early assists," to the exclusion of possibly superior submissions by authors better established. But that would be like betting all the horses in a race; his winnings wouldn't pay his expenses. Furthermore, it would be abandoning a cardinal principle in the *Schooner*'s editorial policy.

Just as Wimberly has tried not to let the place of origin influence his reception of a manuscript, so has he tried to ignore the name of its submitter. He attempts always to appraise the manuscript in isolation from such details.[10] This means that the unknown writer competes as far as possible on equal terms with the well established. While he is not penalized for his lack of reputation, neither is he accorded advantage for his greater need. Consequently, Wimberly has accepted manuscripts from many writers whose reputations at the time hardly seemed to need the boost that publication in the *Schooner* could provide: David Morton, Kenneth Patchen, Peter Viereck, Harold Vinal, Oscar Williams, and Tennessee Williams, to name a few. And under the same policy, Wimberly has frequently returned manuscripts to writers of some reputation: Grace Stone Coates, August Derleth, Robert Erisman, Emmett Gowen, Raymond Kresensky, Arthur H. Nethercot, José Garcia Villa, and others.

Wimberly's attempt to ignore names and reputations is subject to attack from either side. The beginner's advocate may, if he has no magazine to lose, argue that it is not sufficiently generous toward the unknown writer; the business manager, that it is too generous. Wimberly, however, is firmly convinced that his course is the only fair and sensible one. It not only enables the *Schooner* to carry what are in Wimberly's opinion the very best contributions available to it, but it gives to every writer an opportunity to test his work against that of other writers both known and unknown. By adhering to this policy of appraising the manuscripts impartially, then, Wimberly feels that he lends to publication in the *Schooner* a significance which it might otherwise lose.

---

[10] Wimberly is more likely to be influenced by the author's name in the case of non-fiction prose than in the case of the more purely literary submission. Following an eclectic policy, he receives essays and articles on a wide variety of subjects. He hasn't the time or editorial help necessary to check the accuracy and authenticity of all such submissions. So, to avoid possible repercussions from publishing a fraudulent or inaccurate article, he favors those writers who have established reputations or whom he knows personally.

Those writers, new or established, who gain Wimberly's final nod receive for their efforts not one cent in cash. Financially they have lost the value of their time, materials, and postage. Their only tangible returns are, for prose contributions, two copies of the *Schooner* carrying their work, or, for poetry, one. What has led the 1,080 *Schooner* contributors to spend time, labor, and money securing publication in a magazine which pays them nothing for their acceptable work?

In the case of the novice, the answer to that question is reasonably obvious. He feels that he is potentially a writer, and he is struggling for any entree into the field. He has heard from those who know, or more probably he has learned through personal experience, that the few paying markets which use his type of material are so heavily supplied with "sure things" that they have neither time nor motive for considering unknown quantities. He knows, on the other hand, that competition for space in the little magazine is quantitatively less severe, and that his unknown name will not there be a handicap. He knows further that even if he is not published, he can expect from the little magazine editor an honest appraisal of his work, and professional advice and assistance which he could obtain nowhere else. And if he is acquainted with the current literary situation, he realizes also that publication in a reputable little magazine can have an ultimate value far exceeding the highest financial payment he could expect from a commercial market—that it might unlock the door to a book publisher's inner office; that it may lead to his being anthologized; that it is likely to win him a rating in an award annual; and that it is certain to place his name and his work before those by whom literary reputations are established and promoted.

With the better established writer the desire for *Schooner* publication is less urgent, but the motives may be much the same. Few writers become so well satisfied with their reputations that they decline to seek further recognition; and the

publishing writer is, even more than the novice, aware that
the little magazine is the literary man's magazine—that though
its readers are few, they are select and include the publishers
and critics by whom reputations are influenced. If, then, he is
financially able to give away his products, he may be happy to
see them in a little magazine like the *Prairie Schooner*. Warren
Beck, for example, in offering some stories for publication,
wrote (May 5, 1947): "It's out of the little magazines that
my work has found its way into the anthologies."

Then too, the man who has made writing his profession is
eager to see as much of his work in print as is possible. He
may have established a ready market for his stories or poems,
but no magazine, paying or otherwise, is going to overload itself with material under one author's name. So if the writer
is prolific, he is forced to place much of his work in the little
magazines. This probably accounts in part for August Derleth's having returned so frequently to the pages of the
Schooner.

Again, the writer who sells most of his work to commercial
publishers may occasionally write a story which is unacceptable
to them, not because it is a bad story but because it violates
their editorial policies. If the writer thinks enough of the
story, he tries to place it in a magazine where commercial considerations do not greatly influence editorial policy. Thus
R. Balfour Daniels wrote, February 27, 1934:

> After writing a story that violates almost all the
> well-known taboos, one sometimes wonders what to do
> with it. In the present case of "An Evening Call" [pub-
> lished Spring, 1934, as "Muscling in on Mr. Jellifer"]
> I could not help thinking of the *Schooner* because: its
> editor is not afraid of satire, there are no advertisers to
> offend, and there doesn't necessarily have to be any
> woman interest.

An extreme case is that of Paul Ellerbe, whose "Cleaning
Woman" (written in collaboration with his wife) was pub-

lished in the Fall, 1946 issue. The story had been written nineteen years before, when the Ellerbes were receiving $900 a story from *Collier's Weekly*. During those nineteen years it had been submitted to and rejected by forty-one magazines. After Wimberly's acceptance, Ellerbe wrote (April 13, 1945): "It is the kind of thing a commercial fictionist should never write, and we knew that when we wrote it, but I intend always to do a few of them—just as we always did a few of them together—for the best reason in the world—because I want to."

Finally, some of the contributors to the *Schooner* have sought publication there because of a special esteem for the magazine or a sentimental attachment toward it. Hannah Kahn, when she placed a poem in the *Schooner* after having submitted work for some five years, wrote (October 12, 1944):

> Many years ago, long before I started submitting poetry to magazines, Prairie Schooner had a special significance for me because of a story that I read in the O'Brien Short Story collection."

Josephine Johnson of Norfolk, Virginia, on her first acceptance by the *Schooner*, wrote (March 1, 1941):

> I am looking forward with great pleasure to appearing in *Prairie Schooner*. The western magazines have a flavor all their own. I don't mean simply regional (though I like regionalism) but a quality which in a person I should call a quiet self-reliance, never shrill or brittle, which appeals to me immensely.

Tom Bair, on his fourth appearance in the *Schooner*, expressed a similar attitude (May 8, 1951):

> I am always proud to appear in "The Prairie Schooner," not only because I admire the magazine generally but because it somehow always seems to strike just the right note with me where so many of the current magazines slip off toward either academicalism or popular demand.

And Jesse Stuart, twenty years and thirteen books after his discovery by the *Schooner,* wrote (October 23, 1950):

> I thought I should be back with you with a story. So I sent you one of the best I had, if not the best—that will be for you to judge—and you accepted so I'm glad to be back in Prairie Schooner. So it's coming home. Back to the bedrock beginning.

Letters like that may be regarded as an indication of the sentimentality of which contributors to the *Prairie Schooner* are occasionally guilty. But there is little doubt that underlying such letters is a real appreciation of the kind of magazine the *Schooner* tries to be, and, more specifically, a deep and genuine gratitude for the service the *Schooner* has rendered to writers in search of a market.

7

The Schooner *and Its Contemporaries*

At the time of the *Prairie Schooner's* founding, its editors had little sense of association with other elements in the American publishing scheme. They were, indeed, motivated in part by resentment of a scheme which they felt discriminated against writers from their region. But before their magazine was many issues old, its editors had become aware of a kinship with certain other magazines similar to the *Schooner* in objectives, type, and scope—especially with John T. Frederick's *Midland* and H. G. Merriam's *Frontier*. The three magazines resembled one another in several important respects. All were non-commercial, and each emanated from a university campus (the *Midland* from the University of Iowa, the *Frontier* from the University of Montana). Each was more or less regional both in its editorial policy and in its list of contributors. And all three attempted to present a balanced fare of fiction, poetry, articles, and essays (though the *Frontier* printed a larger proportion of essays and articles than did either of the other two magazines).

The names of the three magazines were perhaps first linked by Edward J. O'Brien. In a letter to Wimberly dated May 21, 1929, O'Brien remarked that the *Schooner* "ranks with the

Midland, the *Frontier,* and not more than one or two other American periodicals, as the most significant expression of American life which we possess. As such, it focuses the whole cultural life of a section of America." In the preface to his *Best Short Stories of 1930,* he expanded his remarks:

> In conversation the other day with Mr. Edward Garnett, I had occasion to remark that an English observer, who sought to discover what the significant American note of the new generation was like, would do well to turn his attention to three periodicals of small circulation published in the Middle West,—*The Midland, The Prairie Schooner,* and *The Frontier.* In these three periodicals most of the significant new American prose writers first appear. It is in these pages that you will find the significant American novelists and short story writers of the next twenty years, so far as these writers are indigenous and spring from the soil.

In the same preface, O'Brien made the rather startling suggestion that the three magazines merge to create one large periodical. He pointed to what he considered the inadequacy of the existing quality magazines, indicating that they printed only the "most competent second-best" of American writing, and then continued:

> The true remedy for this lagging behind of the better monthlies is probably the establishment of a new national monthly in the Middle West which is nearer the present centre of population. If I may venture a suggestion, I think the time is now ripe for the *The Midland* to pool its interests with *The Prairie Schooner, The Frontier,* and perhaps one or two other regional periodicals such as *The Southwest Review,* and to issue a full-grown national monthly of belles-lettres in which short stories, poems, and essays should be given pride of place.

The suggestion took Wimberly completely by surprise. His *Prairie Schooner* had just begun to gain real momentum, and he was disinclined to collapse it through a merger. Furthermore, he realized the difficulty of publishing a magazine, even on a small scale, without a great deal of financial backing. He feared that the three magazines combined would lack the necessary resources to compete on a large scale with the well established quality magazines of the day, and that any attempt to do so might result in the death of all three magazines. And certainly his experience with contributors to the *Schooner* had indicated that America needed more magazines willing to print high-quality writing, not fewer. His reply to O'Brien's suggestion was carried by the *Daily Nebraskan*, October 29, 1930:

> I do not believe this is feasible at the present time because competition is too great and because of the financial problem. Likewise, the combined magazine would lack the individuality and character of the separate institutions. However, the suggestion of Mr. O'-Brien's is a good one, and perhaps, in the future something of this sort will be done.

Nothing came of the proposed merger. In the months that followed, Frederick alone tried to carry out a portion of O'Brien's suggestion. In October he moved his *Midland* to Chicago and attempted to expand its appeal. In May of 1931 the magazine began appearing monthly, in a new two-column format.

By this time Wimberly was well aware of the *Schooner*'s kinship with the *Midland* and the *Frontier*. Through correspondence he had established cordial relations with both Frederick and Merriam, and he had cooperated with them in a variety of ways, to be discussed later in this chapter. So, although he had declined to pool his interests with Frederick's, he took friendly note of the *Midland*'s expansion, in the "Ox Cart" for Summer, 1931:

> The editors of the *Prairie Schooner* take this opportunity to congratulate the *Midland* upon its initial

appearance as a monthly.[1] . . . The *Schooner* can in all
sincerity wish the *Midland* Godspeed, for the two magazines have much in common—this particularly as re-
gards their main objective, that of encouraging and developing the literary talent of the Midwest.

In less than two years, however, Wimberly's earlier fore-
bodings concerning the "financial problem" were borne out
by Frederick's experience. After reaching a peak of 1,200, subscriptions to the *Midland* began to drop with the depression in
1931. Despite the magazine's reversion from a monthly to a
bi-monthly, it lost about a thousand dollars a year through
1931 and 1932. And by early 1933 Frederick realized with
reluctance that he could no longer continue.

On this occasion Wimberly again had a chance to combine
his *Schooner* with another little magazine, though this time on
considerably different terms. Early in May of 1933, Frederick
telegraphed asking whether the *Schooner* would absorb the
dying *Midland* by taking over its unexpired subscription list.
Wimberly was aware of the honor conferred by Frederick's
invitation, but he was concerned over the moral responsibility
which would be involved by his accepting. The *Schooner* itself was in immediate danger of collapse. It had just been
forced to cut to about a third of its ordinary size, and even
then it was doubtful that another issue would appear. Its
continuation depended upon favorable action by the university
budget committee. Wimberly was naturally reluctant to accept from Frederick responsibilities which he might not be able
to fulfill; he had too much respect for the *Midland* to serve
it in such a fashion. He wrote to Frederick, requesting time
to consider. On May 16, Frederick replied:

---

[1] Actually the *Midland* had operated as a monthly, though on a smaller
scale, from 1915 to 1928, except for the years 1918 and 1919, when it
appeared bi-monthly, and 1925, when it appeared semi-monthly.

I want to make an announcement as to the unpaid subscriptions in the final issue of the magazine, which I am hoping to have in press by a week from today.

I shall be very glad to hold it up a day or two if necessary, however, in order to give time for hearing from you. I am very glad that my suggestion appeals to you, and hope with all my heart, both because of the *Midland* subscribers and for its own sake, that the *Prairie Schooner* can be continued.

I sincerely believe that our unexpired subscriptions would mean a considerable number of permanent subscribers for you. The few which are left on our list are people who are intensely loyal to the regional magazine idea, and while no doubt some of them already are on your list, I believe there will be a considerable number who do not now know the *Prairie Schooner,* and will learn to like it if they receive a few copies.

During the week that followed, Wimberly tried to get from Chancellor Burnett some assurance that the university subsidy for the *Schooner* would be continued. But with the heavy demands for a cut in the budget, such assurance was impossible. Wimberly advised Frederick to that effect and received his reply, dated May 22:

Thanks for your note as to how the situation has been going. I hope so much that you can arrange to go on, and will appreciate your letting me know at the earliest possible moment.

I am holding the issue, and will have to initiate other arrangements if ours cannot go through.

On the day of that note from Frederick, Merriam of the *Frontier* wrote Wimberly a letter which is interesting not only because it indicates that the *Frontier* and the *Schooner* had common problems and demonstrates the close cooperation between their editors, but also because it contains a hint as to what kind of arrangements Frederick would be able to initiate.

I appreciate your cordial letter of May 16. . . . I sincerely hope that *Prairie Schooner* will be sufficiently subsidized by the University of Nebraska so that it can continue. Would letters from outside your state concerning the value of your magazine, addressed to some University administrator, help or injure your cause? I would undertake to get a few letters—for example, from myself, Mrs. Coates, Albert Wetjen, and others. I feel sure that Mr. Frederick would be willing likewise to send a note.

I wish the *Frontier were* "on a sound basis"; the sad fact is that on June 1 we shall be approximately $500 in the red. But since that is about the sum we were in the red last June I am not worrying—as long as the printers do not push too hard for their money. Last year we put on a Gaiety Night during the summer session and made about $250 for the *Frontier*. Might not you be able to do something like that, if it doesn't seem too undignified in a much larger institution, for the *Prairie Schooner*?

Should you be obliged to discontinue the *Schooner*, would you give the *Frontier* first chance at the use of your subscription list? We would be willing to give you a percentage on every *Frontier* subscription obtained from a *Schooner* subscriber, so that you would be helped in making up arrears or in liquidating. (I hope this paragraph doesn't seem like the bird of prey rushing at a prospective corpse!) I am just about at my wit's end to know how to keep the *Frontier* going.

A few days later Wimberly, still lacking any definite assurance that the *Schooner* would be able to continue, notified Frederick that he would be unable to assume the responsibility of absorbing the *Midland*. Frederick replied, on May 29:

Upon receipt of your telegram Friday I wired Merriam of the Frontier, and have his reply that Frontier is going on and that he will be glad to take over our unexpired list.

I want to thank you for your willingness to do this good deed, and for your effort to get a decision. I know too well the ways of Deans et al to have any difficulty in understanding the delay. I hope sincerely that you may still be able to keep the Schooner going. If it should prove you can't, would it be convenient to let me know —or the event in either case?

The episode concludes with a letter to Wimberly from Merriam, dated June 21, 1933:

I am still hoping that *Prairie Schooner* will not "go under"; but if it does my effort in editing the *Frontier* will be to cover the mid-west field as well as the northwest. It is probable that the *Frontier* next year will be known as "The Frontier and Midland."

Had Wimberly known in May what he was to learn a month or so later, that the *Schooner* would receive the university aid essential to its continuation, or had he been less cautious about committing himself without such assurance, it is probable that there would be today a *Midland Schooner* or a *Schooner and Midland*. As things worked out, however, the *Schooner* was destined to survive through its first twenty-five years without either absorbing any other magazine or being absorbed itself. This is not to say, however, that the *Schooner* has operated in complete isolation from other magazines throughout those years.

One might perhaps suppose that the nation's several little magazines, in passive competition for the same manuscripts and in active competition for the same readers, would be at best cool in their relations and at worst hostile. One might suppose further that little magazines as a group, having justified their existence largely by decrying the failure of the "money press" to print good literature, might be scorned by commercial publishers. Wimberly has found neither supposition to be correct. On the contrary, it has been his experience that the nation's little magazines, its best commercial magazines, and many of its book publishers together constitute a loosely knit and informal association without officers, dues, or by-laws, but with a great deal of mutual respect and cooperation among its members. This association is advantageous both to the individual magazine and to the writer who contributes to the magazine.

Probably the greatest cooperation is among members of the little magazine group. And the more nearly competitive the magazines appear to be—that is, the closer they are geographically and editorially—the greater the cooperation. The *Frontier* and the *Midland* were only two of many little magazines with which the *Schooner* has enjoyed pleasant and mutually profitable relationships characterized by close cooperation.

One evidence of this cooperation is the frequency with which other magazines have been advertised or announced in the pages of the *Schooner*. Since 1940, the *Schooner* has followed the practice of exchanging advertising space with other little magazines and publishers. The magazines which have cooperated with the *Schooner* in this reciprocal advertising include *Accent, Better English, Compass, Decade*, the *Explicator, Galley, Kavita* (India), the *Modern Language Quarterly*, the *New Mexico Quarterly Review, Palisade*, the *Poetry Chap-Book*, the *Rocky Mountain Review*, the *Southwest Review, Why*, and *Wings*.[2]

In addition to carrying such advertising proper, the *Schooner* frequently mentions or comments on other magazines in its editorial pages. The "Ox Cart" section, which contains notes on the *Schooner*'s contributors, is always liberally sprinkled with the names of other magazines in which those contributors have appeared. Take, for example, two volumes fifteen years

[2] The *Schooner* has also carried exchange advertising from Bruce Humphries, Inc., the Harvard University Press, the Philosophical Library, the Russell F. Moore Company, the Southern Methodist University Press, the Swallow Press, the University of Washington Press, and the Vantage Press. Note that it did not begin to carry exchange advertising until after both the *Midland* (1933) and the *Frontier and Midland* (1939) had ceased publication.

apart, chosen at random: the fifth (1931) and the twentieth (1946). In the volume for 1931, a depression volume in which the space devoted to the "Ox Cart" was considerably restricted, fourteen little magazines are mentioned. In that for 1946, twenty-eight such magazines are mentioned, eleven of them more than once, and three of them (*Accent, Poetry,* and *Voices*) as many as five times.

As a rule, the magazines are merely mentioned, but not infrequently the name of a magazine is accompanied by some descriptive or commendatory phrase such as "*Nativity,* a new magazine," "that first-rate magazine the *University Review,*" or "*Voices,* probably the most outstanding verse magazine in America." And occasionally Wimberly has devoted considerable space in the "Ox Cart" to detailed notices of other little magazines. Thus the section for Summer, 1934, opened with the following remarks:

> The *Schooner* is happy to bring to the attention of its women writers the following announcement by the *Spinners,* A Bi-Monthly of Women's Verse: [There follows a hundred-word announcement submitted by Tooni Gordi, editor of the *Spinners.*]
> Excellent literary magazines continue to spring up, their purpose being, in large measure, to supply a place for the work of the relatively unknown but competent writer. Two of the newer literary magazines are *Direction* (Peoria, Illinois) and the *New Tide* (5930 Franklin Ave., Hollywood, Calif.). The editors of these two periodicals invite *Schooner* authors to submit work to them.

And in the issue for Fall, 1938, Wimberly published an extended discussion of current markets for good literature, in which he recommended that writers try such magazines as *Frontier-Midland, American Prefaces,* the *Southwest Review, Tanager,* the *New Mexico Quarterly,* the *University Review,* and *Story.*

Six months later, in the issue for Spring, 1939, Wimberly devoted the first two pages of the "Ox Cart" to a compact but penetrating discussion of little magazines by Weldon Kees. In the article, entitled "Magazine Chronicle," Kees' initial concern was with the many little magazines which had sprung up during the depression years but had since collapsed. Included in his remarks, however, is an extended notice of several little magazines which were still very much alive: the *Southern Review,* the *Partisan Review,* the *Kenyon Review,* and *Twice a Year.* Wimberly appended to Kees' article about a page of his own comments on magazines not covered by Kees' remarks.

On a somewhat larger scale are two well informed and provocative articles by Alan Swallow of the Swallow Press, which were published as regular contributions to the *Schooner*: "The Little Magazines" (Winter, 1942) and "Postwar Little Magazines" (Summer, 1949). Both of those articles display an understanding of and sympathy for the little magazine in general, and the second contains extended descriptions and analyses of several of the leading little magazines of the day. Similar discussions of little magazines occupy the "Midwestern Writers" section in two issues of the *Schooner*. That section for Fall, 1929, is devoted to Martin S. Peterson's "Regional Little Magazines," which is largely a study of the *Midland* and the *Frontier*. And the section for Winter, 1932, contains Mari Sandoz' appraisal of B. A. Botkin's *Folk-Say.*

A special device for advertising other little magazines and their contributors was the poetry reprint section "Crossroads," which, with occasional interruptions, was a regular feature of the *Schooner* from the issue for Winter, 1929, through that for Spring, 1938. The purpose of the feature is indicated in a note which accompanied each appearance:

> This page is the *Prairie Schooner*'s challenge to those who think that the small magazine which does not pay for verse never publishes material which is worth while. Its selections are made only from those smaller literary magazines which are unable to pay for contributions.

During the nine years that "Crossroads" appeared in the *Schooner,* it carried thirty-one poems. They represent the work of twenty-nine poets and were taken from sixteen different sources: *American Prefaces, Bozart, Folk-Say, Forge, Frontier, Midland, Midwest, Nativity, Nebraska Alumnus, Parnassus, Poetry Digest, Spinners,* the Lincoln *Star, Tanager, Verse,* and *Voices.*

The poems reprinted in "Crossroads" were customarily prefaced by an introductory note, usually commendatory, such as the following:

> Lew Ney's struggling little magazine, *Parnassus,* of New York City, is still very much alive, as we discovered after coming across the following poems in two successive issues. (Winter, 1929).

> Our northern neighbor, *The Frontier* (Missoula, Montana), very often strikes a simple, human note that other magazines are in some danger of losing altogether. ... (Summer, 1929)

> The following poem [Thomas Caldecot Chubb's "Two in Sight of Florence"] has been widely quoted since its appearance in *Voices* in November. Mr. Vinal's magazine deserves the support of all poetry lovers. Laboring under financial difficulties which seem to beset all magazines devoted to the Muse, it has refrained from the undignified and shady "rackets" to which certain poetry publications have descended, and at the same time maintained a high standard of accomplishment. (Winter, 1930)

> Selections from the *Midland* are difficult these days. Mr. Frederick is publishing so much verse of quality that choices are bound to be slighting to others. The following poem [Frederic Cover's "Earthborn"] is noticeable for its sincerity and strength. (Fall, 1930)

Such notices in the "Ox Cart," in contributed articles, and in "Crossroads," while advertising other little magazines and their contributors, served also to cement relationships between the *Schooner* and other magazines in the field.[3] They were thus both symptomatic of and conducive to the cooperation which has characterized the activities of America's little magazines and has contributed to their combined importance on the American literary scene.

A look at the *Prairie Schooner*'s list of contributors reveals another important point of contact among little magazines —the contribution of manuscripts by one editor to the journal of another.

With the *Schooner,* this potential avenue of cooperation has been largely a one-way street. During the *Schooner*'s first twenty-five years Wimberly contributed (apart from "Ox Cart" comments) only four stories and fourteen essays to the pages of his own magazine.[4] During that same time, he contributed only two stories and two articles to other little magazines. This despite the fact that his fellow editors frequently addressed to him requests like the following:

> I've been wondering if you'd send us something. We want to make this a first-rate little magazine, and we're casting about for first-rate material. (Roderick Lull, the *Outlander,* December 16, 1932)
>
> If you or any of your friends wants verse or prose in this promising new magazine . . . by all means forward the stuff to me. (Kerker Quinn, *Literary Arts,* October, 1933)
>
> Frankly, I am writing to ask whether you have anything you care to send us. . . . If you have anything at all you care to give us, we shall be glad to have it and thank you devoutly for it. (Leonard Brown, *Avenue,* March 2, 1934)

[3] Wimberly commented in the "Ox Cart" for Spring, 1929, "Through this section [Crossroads] the *Schooner* has already established genial contacts with a number of other magazines."

[4] See p. 26, n. 4. Four of Wimberly's *Schooner* articles appear under pseudonyms. The reason for his contributing so many more articles than stories to the *Schooner* is largely that the magazine is more often in need of articles than of fiction.

If you have the time or the inclination we would be delighted to have you do an article for us. Emboldened by my preceding proposal I may as well now broaden my invitation to be all inclusive and ask you whether you have a story which you would be kind enough to let us publish. (Jay Harrison, *Kosmos,* February 14, 1935)

Don't forget we're still hoping you'll find time to do us a story some time! I've seen a number of your things I liked exceedingly. (Karlton Kelm, *Dubuque Dial,* March 3, 1935)

Wimberly's failure to respond to such invitations by contributing his work was occasioned neither by a lack of ability nor by a lack of interest. He deeply regrets the fact that he has been unable to publish more widely—not only because he feels a bond with other editors of little magazines and would like to have complied with their requests but also because, like most little magazine editors, he is aware of his power to create as well as to edit, and would like to have established a reputation as an author in his own right. The reason that he has not done so is that he has never had sufficient time. He has taught a full schedule of courses not only through the regular school year but through nearly every summer since he joined the staff at the University of Nebraska. This load, coupled with the demands of his job as editor, has left him with neither the hours nor the energy essential to writing much of his own. The stories which he has produced have almost without exception been sold, on their first submission, to one of the quality magazines such as *Harper's* or the *American Mercury.* The following note from H. L. Mencken, dated July 1, 1933, indicates the manner in which Wimberly's contributions were received in the office of the *Mercury:*

Needless to say, I'll be delighted to print "The Cook at Drixall's." It seems to me to be an excellent story. My very best thanks. The usual proof and check should reach you within a week.

The occasional check was, of course, a welcome sight to a man who was trying to rear and educate a family of four children. As long as he could sell his few stories at the level of *Forum, Harper's,* and the *American Mercury,* Wimberly felt compelled to decline invitations to contribute to the various little magazines. Those were not the only invitations he was forced to decline. Alfred A. Knopf (publisher of the *American Mercury*) wrote to Wimberly two days after Mencken's acceptance of "The Cook at Drixall's": "I revert again to our correspondence of something over a year ago and wonder if by now you have a novel in hand. Certainly you could do a good one and I hope you will."

Although Wimberly has been unable to contribute work to other little magazines, he has printed a great many contributions from other editors. The list of contributors to the *Schooner* during its first twenty-five years includes the names of fifty-nine persons who have been connected in an editorial capacity with at least one little magazine. A few of these fifty-nine have served on the staffs of several magazines.

The first of these persons to appear in the *Schooner* was Nebraska's Professor Hartley Burr Alexander, who, while associate editor of the *Midland,* contributed to the *Schooner* four poems, which appeared in the issue for July, 1927. This, however, appears to have been merely a token contribution, a sort of *bon voyage* gift to the infant magazine. Alexander was not so important either to the *Schooner* or to the history of the little magazine as were several others who followed him.

The *Schooner* contributor who has been perhaps most active in little magazine circles is Norman Macleod, whose first *Schooner* poem appeared in Spring, 1929, while he was editing *Palo Verde* (originally called *jackass*). In 1929, while launching his second magazine, *Morada,* Macleod sent Wimberly another poem and inaugurated an exchange subscription, remarking: "We . . . can only hope that before we have finished we shall have accomplished as much for the Southwest and its articulation with the rest of the world as has the *Prairie Schooner* for its section of the country." Since that time Macleod has served as editor of *Calendar* and the *Maryland Quarterly,* associate editor of *Upward,* the *Left,* and the *New Masses,* contributing editor of the *Latin Quarter-ly, Literary Arts,* and the *American Spectator,* foreign editor of *Front,* and advisory editor of *Mosaic.* During the years 1929 through 1939 he appeared in five issues of the *Schooner,* in addition to one reprint in "Crossroads."

Another *Schooner* contributor is Harold Vinal, editor of *Voices* since its first appearance in 1921 and a considerable poet in his own right. His introduction to the readers of the *Schooner* was through a poem reprinted from *Parnassus,* which appeared in "Crossroads" for Winter, 1929. The next issue carried two poems which he had contributed directly, and from that time on he has been one of the *Schooner's* most frequent contributors. Poems by him appeared in twenty-five of the seventy-two issues beginning with that for Spring, 1929.

Nearly as frequent a contributor has been Stanton A. Coblentz, energetic editor of *Wings.* He made his first appearance in the *Schooner* with a poem in the issue for Spring, 1933, at about the same time that his own quarterly of verse first began to appear. Over the next eighteen years, he contributed eighteen poems and six essays to the pages of the *Schooner.*

The *Schooner* carried the first published story by Kerker Quinn, who has served on the staffs of *Direction* (Peoria), *Midwest,* and *Literary Arts,* and who has rendered modern literature a real service with his excellent quarterly *Accent.* Alan Swallow, of the *Rocky Mountain Review,* the *Swallow Pamphlets, Modern Verse,* and the *New Mexico Quarterly,* made his first *Schooner* appearance as an undergraduate at the age of twenty-two. Others among the fifty-nine editors of little magazines who have appeared in the *Schooner* include: B. A. Botkin (*Folk-Say, Space*), Grace Stone Coates (*Frontier*),

Albert E. Clements (*Nativity, Anvil*), Miriam Allen deFord (the *Coast*), Grace Hunter (*Tanager*), Joseph Joel Keith (*Compass*), Karlton Kelm (*Dubuque Dial*), Raymond Kresensky (*Midwest, Hinterland*), Meridel LeSueur (*Midwest*), James F. Lewis (*Crescendo, University Review*), Roderick Lull (*Outlander*), Frank Luther Mott (*Midland*), Winfield Townley Scott (*Smoke*), George Snell (*Rocky Mountain Review*), Upton Terrell (*Earth*), José Garcia Villa (*Clay, Kosmos*), Ray B. West (*Rocky Mountain Review*), and Oscar Williams (*Rhythmus*).[5]

The contributions from editors of other little magazines have benefited the *Schooner* in two ways. They have, of course, helped maintain the quality of the magazine's contents. They have also strengthened the *Schooner*'s contacts with other magazines, thus making more secure its position in the publishing scheme. The relationship between a writer and a magazine which has carried his work is a peculiar one; publication creates a sentimental bond becoming at times an almost proprietary interest on the part of the writer. One good indication of this interest is the large number of letters which Wimberly received from former contributors during the depression of the 1930's, when it seemed that the *Schooner*'s collapse was imminent. Even those who had contributed to the *Schooner* only once or twice indicated a real concern over the fate of the magazine. Typical of the reactions are those expressed in the following comments:

Here's hoping you manage to pull the Schooner through the financial storms. It's needed. It has an air of permanence and solidity that few of the little magazines are ever able to attain. And the way the non-commercial reviews are passing to Valhalla now it looks as

[5] Editorship of another little magazine has not guaranteed an author entry into the pages of the *Schooner*. Wimberly, acting in accordance with his general policy of appraising the manuscript rather than the author's name, has frequently rejected the contributions of other editors.

if it's going to be a sad year for writers. (Roderick Lull, March 7, 1933)

I haven't heard from you about the Schooner. I am praying that it isn't dead. God knows we need the *Schooner*! It seems a crime to have it die. (José Garcia Villa, June 12, 1933)

Such interest on the part of other editors has of course given the *Schooner* a sense of position and purpose.

It is, then, obvious that the mutual interest and respect demonstrated by the editors of little magazines have been beneficial to the individual magazine. Reciprocal advertising, both formal and informal, has served to place the magazine's name before prospective subscribers and prospective contributors. The submission of manuscripts from one editor to another has brought the little magazine much that its editor has been happy to print. And the feeling of membership in a large and vital association, which is engendered by such cooperation, has lent to the individual magazine a sense of significance and strength.

Of more immediate importance to the American writer is still another way in which the little magazines have cooperated. Not only have various editors submitted their own writings to one another, but they have also referred to their fellow editors other writers in search of a market.

One of the biggest problems that Wimberly, or presumably any other editor, has to cope with is his lack of control over the supply of manuscripts. The number and quality of unsolicited contributions, depending as they do on chance and the whims of the contributors, tend to be erratic from issue to issue. Frequently Wimberly has received within a month's time more good publishable manuscripts than the next issue of the *Schooner* could accommodate. Having promised to report within a month and disliking to stockpile manuscripts, he has therefore been forced to return contributions which he would have been happy to print had space permitted. And

again, he has occasionally been forced, for lack of something
better, to print contributions which would not ordinarily
have merited space in the *Schooner*.

Despite the general need for markets willing to print writing of high literary calibre, this temporary dearth of publishable material occurs more widely and more frequently than
one might suppose. It is perhaps most often experienced by
new magazines which are just struggling to become established.
Leonard Brown, in asking Wimberly to contribute to the
newly founded *Avenue*, complained (March 2, 1934): "As you
know, nine-tenths of the stuff that comes in, even to a little
magazine, is unusable. We are sorely in need of short stories
and verse." On March 28 he wrote again, renewing his request
for a contribution from Wimberly and remarking, "It is
much more difficult to find good material than I had ever
supposed."

A similar discovery is described by Robert O. Erisman, in
a note to Wimberly dated May 31, 1933, when Erisman was
preparing the first issue of *Tone*:

> Thank you for returning my manuscripts. Am in-
> deed sorry that the *Prairie Schooner* is uncertain. Your
> advice about most all the literary magazines tottering
> was coincident this morning with my receiving, after
> having notice Sunday of my new magazine *Tone* in
> Sat. Rev. of Lit. & N. Y. Times & N. Y. Herald Tribune,
> just exactly three poems to consider, none of which I
> can use. *Tone* is, or was to be, a magazine of verse, not,
> I hoped, just another magazine of verse, but one in
> which something rich, real, essential would be done with
> poetry. Such wonderful things could be done with it
> that I've always been amazed at the triteness of even
> that that is considered best. I had thought that the
> rich stuff was being ignored by editors brought up on
> anthologies; I begin to see now in a small way that they
> just had nothing better to choose from. Well, here's
> hoping that you can keep the P. S. going; I wish I could
> help you, but my list of subscription prospects has been

successively drained by the *Anvil, 1933,* the *Dune, Forum,* and most recently my own magazine, which I can see now probably won't exist.

And yet, as we have seen, the years in which Brown and Erisman were desperate for publishable manuscripts were two years in which Wimberly, because of the *Schooner's* abbreviated size, was forced to reject much which was well worth publishing. The difficulty, then, is probably not that there are insufficient publishable manuscripts to go around, but rather that they are seldom properly distributed. Obviously it is to the advantage of the little magazine, the little magazines as a collective group, and the writer seeking publication, that each editor operate a sort of clearing house, retaining those manuscripts which he can accommodate and, when overloaded, referring to other markets those competent writers whom he cannot publish at the moment.

It is impossible to estimate the number of manuscripts which have been sent to the *Schooner* at the suggestion of editors of other magazines. An author is naturally reluctant to indicate, on submitting a manuscript to one editor, that it has been previously rejected by another. But there is positive evidence, in the letters accompanying manuscripts sent to Wimberly, or referrals from Karlton Kelm (the *Dubuque Dial*), Harold Merriam (the *Frontier and Midland*), Lucia Trent and Ralph Cheyney (*Horizons*), Jack Conroy (the *Anvil*), and Raymond Kresensky (*Hinterland*). The chances are that those manuscripts which can be positively identified as having been referred to Wimberly by another editor represent only a fraction of those which have actually come to the *Schooner* by that route.

At any rate, Wimberly has worked actively in helping the authors of likely manuscripts to reach a potential market. On January 5, 1933, J. Louis Stoll wrote to Wimberly:

It has been a long time since I have last written you. Several of the would-be's in Philly are getting together

to put out a year book to be called 1933 sometime later
in the year and are looking for unpublished writers for
their material. Perhaps, since you get so much stuff,
you would be nice enough to reroute some of the stuff
our way, to the above address. Thanks an awful lot
for anything or notice you'd care to give us.

In the upper left-hand corner of the letter is Wimberly's
penned reminder to himself:

New Yearbook
Philadelphia
Refer writers to it.

That he did so is indicated by another note received from Stoll
about a month later: "Thanks an awful lot. Got something
the other day through your recommendation. Anything else
you'll turn my way would be appreciated—honest."

Wimberly has cooperated similarly with the editors of
many other little magazines, including, for example, Leonard
Brown of *Avenue,* Robert Erisman of *Tone,* Roderick Lull
of the *Outlander,* Harold Merriam of the *Frontier,* and Alexander Godin of *Dynamo.*

In referring writers to other magazines, Wimberly has been
motivated not only by an interest in those magazines, but by a
desire to help writers in whom he sees some promise. For that
reason he has not referred potential contributors exclusively
to other little magazines. Upon receiving a manuscript which
he can't use but which might well fit into the pages of a commercial magazine, he has often suggested that the writer try
a paying market. He has frequently urged a writer to submit
work to one of the quality magazines such as *Century, Scribner's, American Mercury, Forum, Harper's, Atlantic,* or *Bookman.* And among the magazines of lesser pretensions to which
he has referred writers are the *Saturday Evening Post* and
Nelson Antrim Crawford's *Household Magazine.*

Such referrals of course help to bridge the apparent gap between the American little magazine and the commercial publisher. Actually, however, that gap has perhaps never been so broad as the members of either camp at times pretend. Ellington Curtis, former editor of *Lance,* wrote to Wimberly on May 5, 1936:

> The copy of the Schooner you so kindly sent me some time ago has long been filched by Cincinnati editors, who, by the way, affect much contempt and scoffing at the littles, but forever plague me for copies I might "spare"; and what I send them is read of course, going from hand to hand. When cornered with this, they mumble something about their interest being "academic" and change the subject.

The interest which many editors of commercial magazines show in the little magazines is confessedly not merely "academic." On May 14, 1930, when the *Schooner* was barely three years old, the *Daily Nebraskan* reported: "Bookman, Scribner's and Century have placed their recommendations upon the Prairie Schooner, often referring manuscripts sent to them to the Schooner for its inspection." Three years later, on April 26, 1933, another news item announced that K. S. Crichton of *Scribner's* had invited Wimberly to "bring any likely looking newcomers to his notice" and that Dorothea Brande of the *Bookman* had "complimented the fiction that the Schooner published." It also cited a letter from H. L. Mencken of the *American Mercury,* who wrote: "Thanks very much for the copy of the Prairie Schooner. I have been going through it with great pleasure, and hope to read all of it. I think that you are doing an excellent job with it." In 1935 Henry Goddard Leach, editor of *Forum,* wrote the following, which was printed in the *Nebraskan* for May 22: "My hearty congratulations on the splendid piece of editing which the Prairie Schooner represents. I have a copy before me at the moment, and am sending it on to one of my assistants with abundant notation."

The above evidence indicates that the editors of America's quality magazines have been aware of the *Schooner* and that they have been acquainted with its contents. As a result, it has been possible for a writer to come to the attention of those editors by simply appearing in the *Schooner*. On January 2, 1935, a few months after the publication of his story "Water Tower on the Prairie," (Fall, 1934), K. C. Shelby wrote to Wimberly:

> I find I am semi-famous since appearing in *Prairie Schooner*. Charles Angoff of *American Mercury* has asked to see more of my work, repeatedly, as well as George Leighton of *Harpers*. I have had seven letters from *Harpers*. Also one from *North American Review* and two encouragement notes from *Atlantic Monthly*. Of course they didn't send them without first seeing my work. But what I mean, is, they sent nice letters instead of printed rejection slips. Also two of the better little magazines, *Dubuque Dial* and *Direction* have asked me to contribute to their forthcoming issues. I want you to know that all this makes me very happy. It makes me feel that, eventually, I shall be able to write. George Leighton of *Harpers* seems intensely interested in me, so much that his last letter was seven pages— (imagine it)—and said he was going to do all he could to put me over there. I feel I owe a great deal of this to you.

It is of course possible that Shelby, in an attempt to please, overestimated the *Schooner*'s role in establishing his new position. But it is undeniable that commercial publishers have watched the pages of the *Schooner* and have pursued writers whose work there they have admired. This is true not only of magazine editors but of commercial book-publishing firms. On April 14, 1934, Jessica Tower of the D. Appleton-Century Company wrote:

> I'd like very much to get in touch with Richard
> Sullivan, Francis Fuhr, and Edward T. Kaveny. I want
> to know whether they are writing novels, and if they
> aren't tied up with a publisher, I'd like to see them.
> Could you tell me their addresses?
> We are trying to dig up some new talent; among
> other things, some interested in literature rather than
> programs, etc. (though I'd like to find a good prole-
> tarian novel too). But, if you know of anyone to recom-
> mend, I should appreciate hearing of them.

Four days later, before she had received Wimberly's answer to
her first letter, she wrote again, this time asking to get in touch
with E. A. Sullivan, Bennett Wright, Earl Cranston Ewert,
P. M. Sterling, and Harry L. West. She added:

> I hope you don't think me too grasping; luckily your
> interest is short stories and mine, novels. I forget
> whether I explained that I am trying to dig up some
> new talent. I hope and suppose that you are interested
> in new talent too. I certainly would appreciate your
> sending me the addresses of the above, or any others
> you think well of.

Wimberly, far from thinking her "grasping," was pleased
at the opportunity to furnish what information he could
supply. He has always regarded it a primary function of the
little magazine to bring competent writers to the attention of
commercial publishers who may be interested in their work.
It is largely for this reason that each issue of the *Schooner*
carries in the "Ox Cart" notes describing as completely as
possible each contributor's past achievements and future plans.
Although Wimberly has received several other requests
similar to that from Miss Tower, interested publishers more
often use the addresses given in the "Ox Cart" and send their
inquiries directly to the contributor. Thus August Derleth
advised Wimberly, on November 14, 1932: "Holt & Company
wrote for a book, and you will be pleased to learn if I haven't

yet told you, that Simon & Schuster wrote for 'Evening in Spring' after seeing 'Atmosphere of Houses' in the Schooner [Spring, 1932]." [6]

On April 19, 1942, LeGarde S. Doughty wrote: "I have seen many indications that New York publishers are much impressed by *Prairie Schooner*. Perhaps you will remember that one of them (I think it was Doubleday, Doran) wrote to ask if I had any book length material some time after the appearance of my short story 'But It Happened' in the *Schooner* [Summer, 1940]." And the following recent unsolicited letter from Edmund W. Nash of the McGraw-Hill company indicates that book publishers are continuing to watch the *Schooner* for new material:

> Just a brief note to let you know how enjoyable and rewarding we find "Prairie Schooner." I suppose you may have noticed that we have written to a number of your authors, and shall doubtless continue to do so, for I feel that the quality of the work you publish is very much superior to certain magazines of theoretically greater literary pretensions. Good luck to you, and I need hardly add, long life to your magazine. (October 13, 1953)

The most direct attempt to secure new writers from among the *Prairie Schooner* contributors, however, was that made by the Thomas Y. Crowell company. In 1946 the Crowell company, in cooperation with the *Prairie Schooner*, the *University of Kansas City Review*, and the School of Letters of the University of Iowa, awarded two Fiction Fellowships worth $500

---

[6] Derleth later indicated that his contract with Charles Scribner's Sons (initiated with *Still Is the Summer Night* in 1937) resulted from Max Perkins' seeing "Atmosphere of Houses" in the *Schooner*. This delightful essay appears also in the anthology *Prairie Schooner Caravan*. Its history indicates the value to the prospective contributor of faith and persistence. Derleth confessed to Wimberly in a letter dated December 26, 1932, that "a good many magazines turned it down previous to your acceptance."

each, in a competition open to all contributors to either magazine and all members, past or present, of the School of Letters.
The awards, presented on the basis of an outline and four
chapters of a proposed novel, went to Ralph Rundell (*The
Color of Blood*) and Ruth Schellin (*Cut Down Out of Time*),
both *Schooner* contributors.

In both 1946 and 1947 the Crowell company also awarded
Short Story Prizes of $100 and $50 to the writers of stories
adjudged the best published in the *Schooner*. The winners of
first and second prizes respectively were, in 1946, Hal Ellson
("The Frozen Heart") and Lawrence J. O'Brien ("Small-Town
Stories") and, in 1947, Robert Hutchinson ("Lovely Free Gift")
and Alex Austin ("Snow on the Wings").

One further method by which a writer's work in the
Schooner may bring him wider recognition is through reprinting. Editors interested in reprinting keep a close eye on little
magazines, and frequent reprints constitute another important
link between the *Prairie Schooner* and other elements in
American publishing.

The first *Schooner* piece to be reprinted elsewhere was a
poem by Amy Bruner Almy, "Where the Mesquite Grows"
(Winter, 1928), which appeared in the *Literary Digest* for
March 10, 1928. Since that time contributions have been reprinted in a wide variety of publications. One of the most
important types of anthologies to draw from the *Schooner* is
the award annual. Stories from the *Schooner* have appeared
in the O'Brien-Foley volumes of *Best Short Stories* and the
O. Henry Memorial Award anthologies. Both stories and
poems have been reprinted by Alan Swallow in his annual
anthologies entitled *American Writing*. And poems from the
Schooner have frequently made the pages of such annuals as
Thomas Moult's *Best Poems*, Alan Pater's *Anthology of Magazine Verse*, and the University of Pennsylvania's *Poetry Awards*.

Other reprint publications which have drawn more or less
heavily from the pages of the *Schooner* include the *Digest and*

Review, the *Digest Year Book, Fiction Parade, Modern Story Selections,* the *Magazine Digest,* the *Reader's Digest,* and *World Digest.*

And of course *Schooner* contributions have appeared in various book anthologies, including *Prairie Schooner Caravan,* which was edited by Wimberly and made up entirely of selections from his magazine.

Wimberly has kept no record of the requests he has received for permission to reprint, but the total number would undoubtedly be a large one. Some indication is given by the fact that six contributions to the single issue for Winter, 1935, were reprinted within less than a year.[7] Such reprints mean a great deal to the contributor whose work is selected. In the first place, they sometimes bring a check, usually for a nominal amount but in the case of the *Reader's Digest* for as much as $600. The reprint, however, is valued chiefly for other reasons more important even though less tangible. The very fact that a contribution is selected for reprinting is regarded as a sign of merit and is encouraging to a writer seeking confirmation of his talent. And, perhaps most important of all, the reprinting of a contribution multiplies by many times the size of the writer's audience. It is the desire for an audience that has prompted the writer to contribute to the *Schooner* in the first place; if, by virtue of reprinting, the size of his audience is extended, he is of course doubly happy.

The opportunity which Wimberly has had of furthering the careers of aspiring authors, by furnishing them not only an outlet for their work but contacts with other markets and an opportunity to be reprinted, has increased the significance of his work with the *Schooner.*

[7] *Daily Nebraskan,* September 25, 1935.

8

Achievements and Prospects

A YEAR before the *Prairie Schooner* was founded, the British magazine *Criterion* carried the following statement by its editor, T. S. Eliot:

> The existence of a literary review requires more than a word of justification. It is not enough to present a list of distinguished contributors; it is not enough to express a cordial zeal for the diffusion of good literature; it is not enough to define a "policy". The essential preliminary is to define the task to be attempted, and the place which may be occupied, by any literary review; to define the nature and the function. Many reviews and periodicals qualified as "literary" have proved deficient not so much by their failure to carry out their purposes as by their failure to conceive those purposes and possibilities clearly.[1]

In thus focusing on the magazine's purposes and functions, Eliot not only has provided good advice for those who would edit a critical review or little magazine; he has also suggested convenient criteria by which to measure a little magazine's

---

[1] "The Idea of a Literary Review," *Criterion*, IV, 1 (January, 1926).

achievement. His suggestions acquire special significance when directed at the *Prairie Schooner;* for by "purpose" Eliot obviously means editorial purpose, and in the case of the *Schooner,* that purpose is difficult to define.

The founders of the *Schooner* had no doubts concerning the justification for their magazine's existence. They were attempting to supply a literary voice for their region. The magazine's early success demonstrates both the virtue of that purpose and the extent to which it was achieved. When the *Schooner* abandoned conscious midwestern regionalism—or when regionalism abandoned the *Schooner*—the magazine retained to a degree its purpose of encouraging writers from the region. But that is an accident of geographic location, rather than an editorial direction. And in surveying the *Schooner* since about 1930, one is hard pressed to discover what might accurately be called an editorial purpose.

Indeed one distinctive aspect of the *Schooner,* as contrasted with most other little magazines, is that it does not serve as the organ for any political, social, or critical group. One can examine the entire corpus of the magazine without receiving any clear impression of where Wimberly stands on political or social issues of the day; and though one may distinguish certain editorial preferences or prejudices, he does not find that Wimberly is working to move American literature in any specific critical direction. Except for a few almost mandatory taboos, Wimberly's selection of material appears to be governed entirely by considerations of craftsmanship—competence of structure, skill in the use of language, care in conceiving a desired effect, and ability to achieve it. In short, the *Prairie Schooner* does not have an editorial purpose—unless one can define as such its apparent determination not to have one. Instead it is governed by a two-fold practical purpose: first, for the sake of its readers, to maintain standards of literary excellence while publishing a balanced fare of fiction, poetry, and exposition; and second, for the sake of the American writer, to

offer space whenever possible to those whose writing merits
publication, and, when space is not available, to offer encouragement and practical help.

Whether or not Wimberly has been wise in not restricting
his policy more narrowly is a difficult question. Certainly a
little magazine devoted to a cause has a unity, an identity,
which one does not sense in the *Prairie Schooner*. Such a
magazine has also, if its cause is timely, a spirit and a vitality
which inevitably accompany the crusade. Furthermore, a
magazine which serves as the organ of a strong literary movement will normally attract the best writings of men in that
movement, thus tending to insure the quality of its contents.

But literary movements have a way of losing their vitality,
either through the achievement of their ends, or through the
triteness resulting from repetition of their themes—or, as in
the case of the *Schooner*'s worthy original motive, from a combination of the two.

When Wimberly discovered that the *Schooner* had outlived
its original editorial purpose, there were several courses open
to him. He could have killed the magazine and devoted full
time to his own interests. But his energy and his desire to promote good writing would not permit him to abandon the magazine just as it was achieving a position on the publishing
scene. He could have continued to operate within the narrow
confines of a conscious midwestern regionalism. But he would
have watched the *Schooner* deteriorate into a weak and flabby
anachronism. He could have searched out a new and promis-
ing cause with which to ally his magazine. But he was not
compelled toward any such cause; and a literary cause is like
the ministry—one had better not undertake it unless he feels
the call. So he took the only inviting course open to him. He
made the pages of the *Schooner* a repository for the best writing submitted by authors in need of a market. Except insofar
as the point of view may interfere with literary quality, a
writer's political, social, or critical bias has not been a con-

scious determining factor in the reception accorded his manuscript.

One aspect of Wimberly's editorial policy does, however, appear occasionally to transcend his evaluation of the individual manuscript's intrinsic worth. This is his constant attempt to maintain a variety of forms in the pages of the *Schooner*. It seems unfortunate that he has insisted on maintaining a balance of fiction, poetry, and expository prose, for in achieving variety he has sometimes sacrificed quality.

The sacrifice of quality to variety is most often apparent in the essays and articles carried by the *Schooner*. Ironically, this is not so much despite, as because of, the relatively small number of such contributions carried. Non-fiction prose admittedly occupies an inferior place in the *Schooner*. Realizing this, and knowing that many little magazines and most of the quality magazines are more receptive to exposition, writers of essays or articles have not contributed in any quantity to the *Schooner*. Consequently, although Wimberly is often overstocked with good fiction and poetry, he must frequently petition contributions to fill the space he wishes to allot to essays and articles. The result is prose which, while not uniformly bad, is inconsistent in quality. Many of the contributions are well worth the space they occupy—critical essays by Charles Glicksberg, Bruce Waters, Alan Swallow, and Ray B. West; reviews by Weldon Kees and Loren Eiseley; satirical essays by Frederick Howes, Frederick Christensen, and Wimberly; informative articles by Louise Pound and John D. Hicks. But scattered through the volumes one finds other contributions which are recommended neither by their content nor by the skill with which they are executed—pointless and self-conscious personal essays, heavy-handed satires, and pedestrian scholastic articles.

There is no doubt that the inclusion of such exposition has occasionally forced Wimberly to reject fiction and poetry of merit. One wishes, therefore, that Wimberly were less mathematical in his allotment of space to the different genres—that he would publish articles and essays only when their quality seems clearly to merit their inclusion, and that when such contributions do not present themselves, he would fill the *Schooner* with fiction and poetry. For in these two more literary forms, the *Schooner* has generally maintained a high standard of excellence.

The *Schooner* is probably best known for its fiction. Since 1928, when Edward J. O'Brien singled it out as one of the best American magazines publishing short stories, it has consistently been viewed with respect. Of the first one hundred *Schooner* stories O'Brien considered, eighty-four were acclaimed distinctive. Because of subsequent changes in the method of rating employed in the *Best Short Stories* anthology, it is impossible to appraise the *Schooner*'s entire body of fiction in terms of individual ratings. But O'Brien's successor, Martha Foley, has also been favorably impressed by the *Schooner*'s fiction. In her foreword to the anthology for 1950, after sadly noting the suspension of *Story Magazine*, she wrote: "On the balance side, *Prairie Schooner*, founded in 1927 and the longest-lived of our little magazines, continues to flourish and publish distinguished fiction."[2]

The *Schooner* has perhaps never been regarded by O'Brien or Foley as the leading fiction magazine in America. It was shaded in the late 1920's and early '30's by the *Midland*, in the late '30's by *Story*, and in the '40's by *Story*, the *Kenyon Review*, and the *Partisan Review*. But for over twenty-five years it has consistently been regarded as one of the very few leaders in the publication of good fiction. Other anthologists of the short story have similarly displayed a respect for the *Schooner*. The *O. Henry Memorial Award* volume has frequently listed its stories as distinctive and has reprinted a few. Alan Swallow, whose *American Writing* yearbook covered the

[2] *The Best Short Stories: 1950* (Boston, 1950), p. xiv.

years 1942 through 1944 and included both poetry and prose, considered forty-four *Schooner* stories, of which he rated thirty-three distinctive and republished three. Thomas Uzzell, editor of the annual *Short Story Hits* (1932 and 1933) praised the *Schooner* as one of two magazines containing "some of the most impressive exhibits of new writers appearing today."[3]

The *Schooner*'s poetry has brought it less general acclaim than its fiction. That is not surprising, because there have been many more journals of poetry in America than little magazines devoted to the short story. Not only the quality, but the quantity of verse published by those poetry journals has tended to obscure quarterlies which, like the *Schooner*, carry a variety of literary types. Yet in selecting poetry for publication, Wimberly has always had ample manuscripts from which to choose. The poetry which he has printed has been quite consistently competent, and, in spite of the competition, it has been well received. William S. Braithwaite chose a *Schooner* poem (Helene Magaret's "Legs," Winter, 1929) for his *Anthology of Magazine Verse for 1929,* the last of his volumes to appear. Alan F. Pater, who edited four volumes of a similar annual over the years 1935 to 1942, included at least one poem from the *Schooner* in each volume, and three in that for 1936. The magazine is also represented in most of Thomas Moult's *Best Poems* anthologies from 1929 until the series was discontinued in 1942; his *Best Poems of 1942* carries four poems from the *Schooner,* more than were taken from any other American magazine except the poetry journal *Voices,* which is also represented by four. In his three volumes of *American Writing,* Alan Swallow included two *Schooner* poems and rated thirty-seven others as distinctive in quality. The more recent University of Pennsylvania *Poetry Awards: 1949* (edited by Robert Moore) includes five poems from the *Schooner,* the largest number from any one magazine; the volume for 1950 also carries five *Schooner* poems.

[3] *Short Story Hits: 1933* (New York, 1934), p. 346.

Viewing the first twenty-five volumes as one large unit, one can hardly generalize convincingly about the *Schooner*'s quality. It is difficult enough to secure general agreement on the merits of a single story or poem; when one compounds that difficulty by the number of contributions in a single issue and then multiplies it by one hundred, the number of issues, generalization becomes almost impossible. A close study of the *Schooner*'s first twenty-five volumes, however, leaves one feeling that Wimberly has generally succeeded in his search for quality writing. Except for a few articles and essays, the contributions quite uniformly demonstrate a technical competence (which may be attributable in part to Wimberly's careful editing). Furthermore, they seem generally to possess those qualities of sincerity and significance which distinguish the literary from the merely competent. To be sure, one finds an occasional story which appears contrived or a poem which appears merely imitative, and among the articles and essays one frequently detects journalism rather than literature. But such contributions are in the minority. For the most part, the *Schooner* has attracted writers with something to say as well as an ability to say it.

If expressions of praise are any indication, the *Schooner*'s quality has been considerable. Many qualified critics have commented on the magazine's general excellence. Kerker Quinn, for example, has called it "an Olympian god among American journals,"[4] and Jesse Stuart, "one of the finest magazines, judging from a literary standpoint, that there is in this country."[5] John T. Frederick, reviewing the *Prairie Schooner Caravan*, described that anthology as a "truly noteworthy collection of stories, poems and sketches from the files of 'The Prairie Schooner,' the University of Nebraska's admirable literary magazine."[6] And Paul Alexander Bartlett, editor of

[4] Letter, August 25, 1933.
[5] Letter, December 10, 1941.
[6] "I've Been Reading," Chicago *Sun Book Week*, January 23, 1944, p. 7.

the little magazine *Workshop,* wrote: "I can say convincingly that I have the highest esteem for Prairie Schooner; it has shown such excellent taste and genuine literary integrity."[7] Among other critics who have praised the general quality of the *Schooner* are H. L. Mencken, Whit Burnett, Norman Macleod, Mark Schorer, and Frank Luther Mott.

Such praise constitutes a large portion of Wimberly's compensation for his long years of hard work on the *Schooner.* An even greater reward comes in the many expressions of gratitude from writers whose work he has published, and in the realization that by providing a market for their work he has helped to encourage good writing in America. It is not so much that the *Schooner* has "discovered" one writer or another, but that it has given space to more than a thousand writers, nearly all of whom have created something of worth. Many of them have moved on to gain national recognition; but even that larger number who are destined to remain obscure have contributed something toward a definition of the nation's literature.

This broader achievement was emphasized in a description of the *Schooner* which appeared on the dust jacket for the *Prairie Schooner Caravan:*

> The editor, Dr. Lowry Charles Wimberly, insists that the *Prairie Schooner* is strictly amateur. But in its amateurism the magazine has yielded nothing in its demands for literary excellence. In retrospect, this excellence is impressive not only as a factor in stimulating young men and women to write professionally, but also as a means of encouraging hundreds of contributors to write for the sheer pleasure of writing or to give expression to some impulse or mood of the moment.
>
> The *Prairie Schooner Caravan* is presented, therefore, with justifiable pride in such names as those of Jesse Stuart, Mari Sandoz, William March, Warren

[7] Letter, November 12, 1948.

Beck, Eudora Welty, August Derleth, Meridel LeSueur, Weldon Kees, and Albert Halper, but with equal pride in the high quality of writing which came from the pens of men and women who wrote for publication only once perchance, and that time for the *Prairie Schooner*.

It is unfortunate that Wimberly and other editors of little magazines have had to derive their compensation from such intangibles as kind words and a feeling of accomplishment. But it is true that a little magazine's value is seldom reflected in the reception accorded it. One of the most discouraging aspects of the little magazine's plight is inability to secure subscribers. Had the *Schooner* sold one year's subscription to each person who has submitted manuscripts, and had it circulated to no one else, its average paid subscription list would have been more than doubled. The University of Nebraska faculty alone could supply a subscription list which would permanently end the *Schooner*'s financial worries; but in 1953 faculty members who paid over $14,000 to watch Nebraska's losing football team expended less than $50 to read and support the school's little magazine.[8]

In the case of magazines which, like the *Schooner*, are associated with universities, it is also regrettable that more academic recognition does not attach to the position of editor. Edward J. O'Brien wrote, in 1933, concerning the *Schooner*'s value to the university: "It is worth the salaries of twenty instructors, not only from an ideal point of view, but even from the point of viewing prestige."[9] Yet editorship of the magazine carries no salary at all; it does not relieve the editor of any portion of his teaching load, as administrative work does; and it does not contribute toward academic promotion or tenure as does time spent in scholastic research.

[8] As of May 1, 1954, the *Schooner* had a total circulation of only 306 paid subscriptions. The total for the city of Lincoln—including university faculty, staff, and students—was only 45.

[9] *Daily Nebraskan*, April 26, 1933.

In one respect, however—thanks to a few perceptive people in administrative positions—the *Schooner* has fared better at the hands of the University of Nebraska than has the little magazine generally. The school has never failed to provide deficiency appropriations essential to the magazine's continuance. Without such appropriations the magazine would have died long ago, despite Wimberly's best efforts.

As Wimberly approaches the age of retirement, one wonders what will be the eventual fate of his magazine. It will not be easy for the university to find another man of Wimberly's energy and ability who is also so dedicated to the cause of American writing that satisfaction in a job well done obviates the necessity for other compensation. It seems more likely that the magazine will expire when Wimberly ceases to be active. And perhaps such would be the proper course. There is truth in John Crowe Ransom's statement: "When the editorial impulse is spent it seems altogether a mistaken piety to try to 'keep the magazine alive,' as if there were a virtue in the business. It is time then to let nature take its course." [10] Certainly when Wimberly is no longer able to edit the *Prairie Schooner* the editorial impulse which has moved the magazine through most of its career will have been spent.

But if the *Prairie Schooner* does cease publication sometime during the next few years, one hopes that there will be somewhere in the Midwest—perhaps even on the Nebraska campus—another editorial impulse sufficient to produce a magazine to fill the place vacated. The new magazine should not attempt to be the *Schooner,* but should take the direction dictated by its impulse, adding a new name and a new personality to the long list of little magazines which have served to encourage and develop this nation's literature. As long as there are Americans who aspire to literary success, there will be a need for non-commercial little magazines in which they can test their

[10] "These Little Magazines," *American Scholar*, XV, 551 (Autumn, 1946).

talents and establish their competence. If the day comes when we no longer have such magazines, our literature will be the poorer.

APPENDIX

APPENDIX

A

GEOGRAPHICAL DISTRIBUTION OF CONTRIBUTORS

Contributors have been grouped below according to the type of their first contribution and their place of residence at the time of its submission. In nearly all cases the place of residence accepted for this table is that given by the contributor in the letter accompanying his manuscript. Authors of items reprinted in the *Schooner* are not included unless they have also contributed directly.

Place	*Poetry*	*Fiction*	*Exposition*	*Total*
Alabama	1	6	....	7
Arabia	....	1	....	1
Argentina	1	....	....	1
Arizona	1	3	1	5
Arkansas	2	....	1	3
California	63	39	12	114
Canada	3	....	....	3
China	1	....	....	1
Colorado	11	4	5	20
Connecticut	9	2	1	12
Cuba	....	2	....	2
Delaware	....	1	....	1
District of Columbia	6	4	....	10
Dominican Republic	....	1	....	1
Eire	1	1	....	2
England	6	....	1	7
Florida	7	5	5	17
Georgia	4	2	....	6
Hawaii	2	1	....	3
Illinois	12	10	8	30
India	1	....	....	1
Indiana	9	3	1	13
Iowa	15	10	1	26
Italy	1	1	....	2
Kansas	11	3	2	16
Kentucky	3	3	1	7

Place	Poetry	Fiction	Exposition	Total
Louisiana	6	5	....	11
Maine	3	1	....	4
Maryland	7	2	1	10
Massachusetts	11	6	3	20
Mexico	2	....	2	4
Michigan	7	4	3	14
Minnesota	4	7	3	14
Mississippi	2	1	....	3
Missouri	13	3	5	21
Montana	4	1	1	6
Nebraska	115	60	150	328*
Nevada	1	....	....	1
New Jersey	12	5	1	18
New Mexico	1	2	1	4
New York	65	50	11	126
North Carolina	3	5	....	8
North Dakota	1	....	....	1
Ohio	14	3	3	20
Oklahoma	6	4	4	14
Oregon	9	3	....	12
Pennsylvania	10	17	2	29
Philippine Islands	....	2	....	2
Rhode Island	3	1	1	5
Scotland	1	....	....	1
South Carolina	....	....	1	1
South Dakota	3	2	....	5
Sweden	1	....	....	1
Tennessee	3	5	1	9
Texas	9	10	4	23
Utah	3	1	1	5
Vermont	....	1	....	1
Virginia	7	1	....	8
Washington	6	4	1	11
West Virginia	....	2	....	2
Wisconsin	3	8	7	18
Wyoming	2	2	1	5
Unidentified	3	....	1	4
Totals	510	320	247	1,080

* Three Nebraskans contributed plays.

B

LIST OF CONTRIBUTORS

Contributors to the first twenty-five volumes of the *Prairie Schooner* have been listed below, with the number of times each appeared. Figures in parentheses represent the number of times the writer has been *reprinted* in the *Schooner,* in addition to the indicated direct contributions. When a writer has contributed two or more poems to one issue, that has been treated as a single appearance. Regular editorial features such as the "Ox Cart," "Dog in the Manger," or "Bibliana," have not been included as contributions, but signed book reviews have been included. Asterisks indicate pseudonyms.

Abbe, George—3 (1)
Abbott, Delmas Wickliffe—1
Abbott, Keene—1
Abell, Elizabeth—1
*Adam, S.
　See Skapski
Adams, Helen—1
Adams, Marguerite Janvrin—5
　—and Clifford H. Pope—2
Agans, H. G.—1
Akenbrand, Frank, Jr.—(1)
Akins, Exha D.—1
Albee, George—2
Albrecht, Erich—1
Alcorn, Helen—1
Alcorn, Paul—1
Aldrich, Bess Streeter—1
Aldrich, Robert S.—8
Alexander, Eleanor—1
Alexander, Hartley Burr—1
Alexis, Joseph—1
Alldredge, Charles—2
Allen, Elizabeth Herriot—2
Almy, Amy Bruner—4
Alyea, Dorothy—1
Ambrosino, Ralph—1
*Amon, Silas
　See Eiseley
Anderson, Paul D.—1
Andrews, John Williams—1
Angoff, Charles—7
Annixter, Paul—2
Anonymous—15
Appel, Benjamin—1
Arguilla, Manuel E.—2
Armstrong, Elizabeth—1
Armstrong, O. K.—1

Arnold, Nelle—5
Arnold, Thelma M.—1
Asher, Elise—1
Atamian, David—1
Austin, Alex—3
Avrett, Robert—1
Babb, Sanora—2
Bahcall, Harold Rufus
　*Bakalor, Rufus—1
Bailey, Dudley—1
Bair, Tom—4
*Bakalor, Rufus
　See Bahcall
Baker, Glen—1
Baker, James V.—5
Bakjian, Mardie Jay—1
Ballard, Charles—9
Ballinger, Ralphe E.—1
Barber, Solon R.—1
Barnes, Sid—1
Baro, Gene—1
Barron, Eve—2
Barron, James R.—1
Barrowes-Donald, H. C.—1 (2)
Bartlett, Paul Alexander—4
Baughan, Denver Ewing—1
Baxter, Dorothy Nicoll—1
Beath, Paul Robert—1
Beaudoin, Kenneth Lawrence—2
Beck, Warren—4
Beilharz, E. A.—1
Benjamin, Edwin B.—1
Bennett, John Frederick—4
Bennett, Mildred R.—1
Bernstein, David—1
Bertschy, Irene—1
Bestercey, Ilona—4

Bidwell, Martin—1
Bidwell, Walter E.—1
Binney, James—4
Birney, Earle—1
Bishop, Ellen—2
Bittner, Nelson Del—1
Bjornson, Guro—1
Blackstock, Walter—1
Blake, Phil D.—1
Blankertz, Don—4
Blasing, Betty—1
Bleeker, Josephine—1
Bloom, Margaret—1
Bloyd, Levi H.—1
Bock, Frederick—1
Boé, Arnold H.—1
Boggs, Lois H.—1
Boggs, Thomas Bonney—(1)
Bolker, Norman—3
Boone, Jack H.
   —and Merle Constiner—1
Bosch, Juan—1
Botkin, B. A.—2
Boucher, C. S.—1
Bouwsma, O. K.—1
Bower, Donald E.—2
Braddy, Haldeen—1
Bradley, Clarke C.—2
Bragin, Moe—1
*Brander, Elizabeth
   See Gaffney
Brengelman, Fred H.—1
Bright, Verne—2
Broady, Lois Pedersen—1
Brodkey, Elsie—1
Broman, Jessie Goddard—2
Brookhouser, Frank—5
Brooks, Nancy—1
Brossard, Chandler—1
Brothwell, Della—1
Brown, Bob—1
Brown, Harry—1
Brown, Spencer—2
Browne, William Randolph—1
Bryan, Horace—1
Buchanan, Patricia—1
Bucklin, Clarissa—6
Buell, Hester—3
Bukin, Arthur—1
Bullock, Flora—1
Burcham, Mildred—1
Burden, Jean—1
Burnett, Olen W.—1
Burr, Winifred Adams—1

Burrough, L. G.—1
Burwell, Mary—2
Buxbaum, Katherine—1
Byard, Dorothy Randolph—2
Byers, Eleanor—1
Byrne, J. Patrick—1
Byrne, Josephine Louise—1
Byron, Gilbert—1
Byxbe, Lyman—1
Calderwood, Carmeleta—1
Calkins, Alden E.
   —and Waldron Webb—1
Campbell, Rachell Harris—1
Cane, Melville H.—6
Canine, William—1
Cannell, Margaret—5
Caplan, Earl X.—1
Capote, Truman—1
Card, William—1
Carleton, Sara King—3
Carleton, William G.—1
Carlson, Robert E.—2
Carman, Olive—2
Carpenter, Janet—1
Carroll, Walter—1
Carter, Boyd G.—5
Carter, Ross S.—1
Carter, Thomas H.—1
Casteel, John—2
Cather, Willa—(2)
Caukin, Helen Ferguson—1
Chay, Marie—1
Chehonin, Mihail—1
Chen, Kwei—2
Cheney, Rowena—3
   *Barbara Hollis—1
Cherwinski, Joseph—3
Chew, Byron—1
Chino, R. Asahai—1
Christensen, Frederick L.—16
Christman, Berniece Bunn—2
Chubb, Thomas Caldecot—(1)
*Church, Jerry
   See Kearful
Churchman, Evelyn—1
Clarenbach, Fred A.—1
Clark, L. B.—1
Clark, Mary Gail—1
Clark, O. M.—1
Clark, W. Edward—1
Clarke, Desmond—5
Claytor, Gertrude—2
Clements, Albert Edward—4 (1)
*Clements, R. S.—1

Clough, Wilson O.—4
Coakley, Frances—1
Coates, Grace Stone—1
Coblentz, Stanton A.—24
Cochran, Joseph—1
Coffee, John T., Jr.—1
Cohen, Nathan—1
Colburn, Dorothy J.—1
Coleman, Lucile—1
Compton, Nellie Jane—5
Connor, Carol C.—1
Constiner, Merle
    See Boone
Cook, Dorothy—2
*Cook, Frank
    See McGovern
Cook, R. L.—2
Cooper, Billy B.—5
Corey, Stephen M.—1
Coristine, Alwyn—1
Corle, Edwin—2
Corning, Howard McKinley—1
Cosgrave, Pearl Joan—1
Cosgrove, Elizabeth W.—1
Coty, Elizabeth—1
Cover, Frederic—(1)
Cowley, Joseph G.—1
Cox, Annis—4
Cox, Florence Louise—1
Cox, James E.—3
Craddock, Edward V.—1
Crawford, Frances-Elizabeth—1
Crawford, Mary M.—1
Crawford, Robert P.—1
Creekmore, Hubert—2
Criswell, Carl S.—1
Criswell, Cloyd Mann—6
Crook, Kile—1
Crouse, Bertha L.—1
*Croye, Eronel
    See Eiseley
Cummings, E.—1
Cummings, Susie Lee—1
Cuneo, James A.—1
Cunningham, Harry F.—1
Current-Garcia, E.—5
Curtis, Christine Turner—4
Curtis, Ellington—1
Daniels, Earl—10
Daniels, Guy—1
Daniels, R. Balfour—4
Darcy, Louise—1
Davidson, Gustav—3
Davis, Eileen—2

Davis, Ercelle—1
Davis, Smith—1
Davis, W. T.—2
Deal, Borden—2
Deasy, Mary—1
Decker, Hermann T.—1
deFord, Miriam Allen—5
DeJong, David Cornel—1
Delaney, Margaret—1
Delehanty, Elizabeth—1
DeLisle, William—6
Delly, Lillian—2
Deming, Horace G.—3
Deming, Joe—2
Deming, Margaret—2
Dennison, Paul—1
DePledge, Orian—1
Derleth, August W.—17 (1)
deVito, Ethel Barnett—1
DeVries, Carrow—2
Dewey, Thomas S.—1
*Dexter, Van Martin
    See Wimberly
Dickson, Lewis M.—1
Dierks, Henry—1
Diers, Theodore C.—2
Diller, Mary Burwell
    See Burwell
Dimmette, Celia—2
Doane, Gilbert H.—4
Donovan, Alan—1
Dorais, Leon—1
Doughty, LeGarde S.—19
Douglas, Gilean—8
Dowling, Albert W.—1
Downey, Harris—1
Dragonetti, Mary—1
Drake, Leah Bodine—1
Draper, E. S.—3
Drath, Francis S.—3
Drewry, Carleton—2
Dreyer, Martin—5
Dugan, Marie—1
Duke, Larry—1
Dunn, Bernice—1
Dunsing, Dorothy—1
Durkee, Caroline Cain—1
Dykeman, Wilma—1
Dykstra, Leslie—1
Eastwick, Ivy O.—5
Eaton, Charles Edward—2
Eckles, Dora Bower—2
Edee, Winifred—1
Edgar, Ruth—1

Edwards, Archibald C.—4
Ehrenberger, A.—1
Eiche, Eleanor—2
Eiseley, Loren C.—31
    *Eronel Croye—1
    *Silas Amon—1
    *Tlo Honda—1
Eisenberg, Frances—1
Eliason, Norman E.—1
Ellerbe, Paul—3
Ellis, Carolyn—5
Ellis, Margaret—1
Ellison, George—2
Ellison, Jessie T.—4
Ellson, Hal—6
Elmore, J. S.
    See Michaelson
Engell, Else—1
Engle, Paul—(1)
Erickson, Saare—1
Erno, Richard B.—1
Evans, Blanche Tromblé—2
Evans, Oliver W.—8
Ewert, Earl Cranston—2
Fader, Garnet N.—1
Fairclough, G. T.—1
Faller, Harold—1
Faulkner, Virginia—1
Feinstein, George W.—2
Fellman, David—3
Ferriss, Jean—1
Fess, Gilbert Malcolm—2
Fichter, Edson H., Jr.—3
Fiegenbaum, Martha—1
Fineman, Morton—1
Firebaugh, Joseph J.—1
Fischer, Mary M.—1
Fisher, Arista E.—1
Fisher, Garland B.—2
Fisher, Hazel—1
Fisher, Phoebe—1
Fitzell, Lincoln—1
Fitzpatrick, Mary L.—1
Flanagan, John T.—1
Flanders, Ruth
    See McNaughton
Flaum, Larry S.—1
Flaum, Salem—2
Fletcher, Lewis—1
Flood, Janet M.—1
Fogel, Ephim G.—1
Folda, Olga—1
Fonda, V. Sheridan—1
Fontaine, Robert—8

Foos, George DeWitt—1
Foote, A. A.—1
Foote, Ellis—1
Forkin, Katherine M.—1
Forward, Kenneth—2
Foster, Harry H.—1
Fraenkel, Michael—1
Fraker, Edward L.—1
Francis, H. E.—1
Francis, Raymond L.—1
Frantz, R. W.—1
Frederickson, Edna Tutt—2
Free, Frederick H., Jr.—1
Freeman, I. H.—1
Friedman, Ralph—1
Friedrich, Ralph—10
Friggens, Paul—1
Frye, Prosser Hall—(1)
Fuhr, Francis—1
Fuller, Ethel Romig—7
Furman, Bess—1
Gable, Jacob H., Jr.—5
Gabrial, Jan—1
Gärtner, Chloe—1
Gaffney, Wilbur G.—15 (1)
    *Elizabeth Brander—1
    *M. R. Lowe—1
Galbraith, Georgie Starbuck—1
Galbraith, Lucretia—1
Galbraith, William M.—6
Gallo, Sam—1
Galloway, Edward—1
Gamboa, Delfin Ferrer—1
Garrick, Jed—1
Garcia Lorca, Federico—1
Garcia Villa, José—5
Gay, Pauline—1
Gegenbach, Gloria—1
Gellert, Minna—1
Genee, Edythe Hope—1
Gerecht, Asher—1
Gerry, W. H.—5
Gerstine, John—1
Gessler, Clifford,—7 (1)
Gettmann, Royal A.—1
Getty, Norris—4
Gifford, Mildred Sparks—1
Gillis, Everett A.—1
Gilman, G. LaSelle—3
Ginsburg, Michael S.—5
Gipson, Eugenia Harriet—2
Giuffra, Madeline—1
Glazer, Tom—1
Glen, Emilie—2

Glenn, Eunice—1
Glicksberg, Charles I.—10
Gluck, Amelia—1
Golightly, Max C.—1
Goodman, Mae Winkler—1
Gordi, Tooni—1
Gordon, Don—1
Gostelow, Willard F.—1
Gowen, Samuel Emmett—1
Graeffe, Arnold D.—1
Graham, Anne Shippen—1
Grandison, Olive—1
Graves, Lloyd Milner—2
Green, E. Sidney—1
Greer, Scott—2
Gregory, Jeanne—1
Griffin, Howard—1
Griffith, E. V.—1
Griffiths, Berta B.—1
Grimes, Eva Miller—1
Grimes, George—2
Grobmann, Edith—4
Grossberg, Paul—1
Grosse, W. Howard—1
Grote, Hed—1
Grubb, Joyce E.—1
*Gulliver
    See Sonderegger
Gunn, Marjory—1
Gunnerson, Dolores—1
Gustafson, Elmer—1
Gustafson, Ralph—1
Guy, Earl—5
*H., J.
    See Stepanek
Hackman, Martha—1
Hadian, Eleeza—1
Halbert, Bernice—1
Hale, Joy—1
Haley, M. Kathleen—1
Hall, Chenoweth—1
Hall, Cora Myra—1
Hall, Frances—1
Hall, Ivan—2
Halliburton, Maurine—1
Halper, Albert—2
Hamil, Harold—1
Hamilton, Horace E.—4
Hamilton, Marion Ethel—1
Han, Chou—1
Hanson, Bip—1
Hanson, Catherine E.—1
Harms, Fred—1
Harper, Carol Ely—1

Harper, Lawrence A.—4
Harries, Eloise Street—1
Harriman, Dorothy—2
Harrison, Paul W.—3
Hart, Mildred Burcham—2
    See Burcham
Hartley, Roland English—1
Hartman, A. H.—1
Hartman, T. H.—1
Haskin, Maribel Coleman—1
Hasley, Louis—2
Haste, Gwendolen—1
Hatchell, Harry—1
Hathaway, Baxter—3
Haughawout, Margaret E.—3
Hausmann, Joy—1
Hawthorne, Worley—1
Hayes, Helen Mary—2
Hayman, Lee Richard—2
Hays, Agee—1
Heath, Monroe—1
Heber, Michael—1
Heineman, Lorene D.—4
Henegan, Herbert—1
Henze, Helen Rowe—1
Henze, Katherine Carr—1
Herndon, Brodie S.—1
Herron, Ruth—1
Hertz, Richard—1
Hertzler, J. O.—1
Hewitt, I. D.—1
Heywood, Terence—1
Hicks, John D.—2
Hicks, Lucile—1
Higbee, Alma Robison—3
Hill, Alma—1
Hills, Barton—3
Himmell, Sophie—2
Hinman, Eleanor—1
Hinz, John P.—1
Hirst, Pauline—2
Hodel, John—1
Hoiberg, Otto G.—1
Holden, Marcia Nichols—1
Holder, Preston—1
*Hollis, Barbara
    See Cheney
Holmes, John A.—(1)
Holmes, Lawrence Richard—1
*Honda, Tlo
    See Eiseley
Hood, Forrest—1
Hoover, Floyd W.—4
Hopkins, Jeannette—1

Horne, Elma Reeder—1
Horowitz, Mort M.—1
House, Richard—4
Howard, Eric—2
Howes, Raymond F.—2
Howson, Margaret—1
*Hudson, Hillary
   See Lodge
Hudson, Hoyt—(1)
Hudspeth, Willis—1
Huerta, Efrain—1
Hughes, Dorothy Berry—2
Hughes, Tom—1
Humbert, Gerald V.—1
Hunt, Hamlen—1
Hunt, Mary Fassett—1
Hunter, Grace—3
Hupp, Alice Hyde—1
Hurd, Harry Elmore—2
Hutchinson, Robert—1
*Hyatt, Dexter—1
Jackson, Evalene Parsons—1
Jackson, George L.—1
Jackson, Margaret—1
Jackson, Russell L.—1
Jacobs, Elijah L.—2
Jarvis, Lavon—3
Jefferey, Mary Louise—1
Jenness, Arthur—1
Jennings, Frances—(1)
Johnson, E. Gustav—1
Johnson, Geoffrey—13
Johnson, Josephine—1
Johnson, Maurice O.—6
Johnston, Laban Thomas—1
Johnston, Marlise—1
Jones, Leila—1
Jordan, Hope Dahle—1
Jorgensen, Helene H.—2
Kadow, August—5
   *August Kateau—2
Kahn, Hannah—1
Kahn, Ralph Anchell—2
Kanfer, Allen—3
Kaplan, Milton—2
Karchmer, Sylvan—1
*Kateau, August
   See Kadow
Kauffman, Bernice—2
Kaufman, Leonard—1
Kaveney, Patricia—1
Kaveny, Edward T.—1
Kayko, Ingeborg—1
Kearful, Jerome

*Jerry Church—1
Kearns, John—(1)
Keefer, George—1
Keen, Raya—1
Kees, Weldon—15
Keith, Joseph Joel—16
Kelley, Glenn Orville—1
Kelly, Maurice—(1)
Kelly, Robert Glynn—1
Kelm, Karlton—1
Kempe, Mary Louise—7
Kennedy, Gerald—1
Kensinger, Faye Riter
   See Riter
Kent, Lucy—1
Kercheville, F. M.—1
Kernan, Plowden—2
Kidd, Walter
   *Conrad Pendleton—9
Kilander, Carl I.—3
King, Ellen—1
Kirk, Russell—1
Kirkpatrick, Doris—1
Kiser, Martha Gwinn—1
Kitchel, Kelsey—1
Kittredge, Herman E.—1
Klein, Alexander—1
Koch, Fred—7
Konecky, Eugene—2
Kopshaw, Charles W.—1
Korb, Ruth—1
Korman, Seymour—1
Kraeft, Norman J.—1
Krenz, Thelma M.—1
Kresensky, Raymond—2
Krieg, Hazel R.—1
Kroll, Ernest—2
Kruger, Fania—1
Kuneticka, Bozene Vikova—1
Kurz, Grace—1
Kurz, Harry—1
Kushner, Shirley—1
Kwiat, Joseph J.—1
Kyle, Homer L.—1
Laidlaw, Clara—1
LaMonte, John—1
Lampson, Robin—1
Lancaster, Lane W.—4
Lang, Varley—1
Langdon, Mabel—7
Langford, Gerald—2
Langland, Joseph—1
Lanning, George—1
Lasch, Robert N.—2

Latimer, Albert—1
Lawson, Clarence—1
Leatherby, James Norman—3
LeClaire, Gordon—1
Lee, Marion—1
Lee, Gretchen—1
Lee, Robert—1
LeGear, Laura Lourene—1
LeGros, Cardinal—1
LeMaster, Catherine—1
L'Engle, Madeleine—1
Lennen, Elinor—1
Lerner, W. Zolley—1
LeRossignol, J. E.—8
LeSueur, Meridel—2
Lewis, Alfred—2
Lewis, Bertram A.—1
Lewis, James Franklin—2
Lewis, Norman Arthur—2
Lindberg, Marcella—1
Lindsay, Charles—2
Linn, Carl—1
Lippincott, Arthur—1
Lister, Queene B.—1
Litsey, Sarah—1
Lloyd, Donald J.—3
Locke, Walter—(1)
Lodge, Rivers—1
　　*Hillary Hudson—1
Longchamps, Joanne de—4
Loos, Laverne—1
Lorca, Federico Garcia
　　See Garcia Lorca
Lord, David—2
Love, Jane Groome—3
*Lowe, M. R.
　　See Gaffney
Lowry, Jan Gabrial
　　See Gabrial
Lugn, Alvin L.—1
Lull, Roderick—5
Lund, Margaret Deming—2
Lund, Mary Graham—2
Lyon, Carrie Ward—1
Lyons, Paul—1
Lyons, Richard—3
Lytle, Marcus Z.—1
McAfee, Tom—1
McCarthy, John Rusell—3
McCord, Fletcher—1
McCulloch, Samuel Clyde—1
McCurdy, Harold Grier—2
MacDonald, Jack—2
　　—and James A. Sheedy—1

*Alan MacDonald—2
McDougle, William Sellars—1
McGovern, Edith E.—1
McGovern, Frank
　　*Frank Cook—1
McKay, Harriet Mills—1
McKenna, Edward L.—2
McLaughlin, Anne—1
McLaughlin, Venard—1
McMillan, Cynthia M.—1
McNaughton, Ruth Flanders—2
McNeil, Ivar Xenophon—1
McPhaul, John J.—1
McRae, Emma—3
Mackay, Margaret Mackprang—1
Macleod, Norman—4 (1)
Macumber, Marie—3
　　See also Sandoz
Maddock, Mary—1
Magaret, Helene—6
Maguire, Francis—1
Maiden, Lewis Smith—1
Main, Joni—1
Maino, Jeanette Gould—3
Mallan, Lloyd—1
Malone, Kemp—1
March, William—4
Marechal, Leopoldo—1
Marinoni, Rosa Zagnoni—1
Marquis, Dorothy—1
Marr, Gaylord—1
Marsh, Robert—1
Marsh, Willard N.—2
Marshall, Lela—1
Martin, George—2
Martin, Mari—2
Martin, Thirza—2
Massier, Elizabeth—1
Masters, Charlie—1
Matthews, Alberta—1
Matthews, Harold J.—1
Maxwell, Cordray—1
Mayhall, Jane—1
Meadows, Paul—4
Mecham, Ada Jean—1
Melick, Weldon—1
Mengers, Marie C.—3
Mengler, Stanley—1
Meredith, Mamie—1
Merrell, Silvia—1
Merriam, Eve—1
Merrill, Herbert—2
*Merriwell, Lathrop Q.
　　See Wimberly

Merryman, Mildred Plew—1
Meston, Leta—3
Metcalf, H. Genevieve—1
Mettlen, Neva Dell—2
Meyers, Burt—1
Michaelson, L. W.
    —and J. S. Elmore—1
Miller, Agnes—2
Miller, Arthur L.—1
Miller, Dick—2
Miller, J. Corson—1
Miner, Virginia Scott—3
Moncure, Peyton—1
Montenegro, Carlos—1
*Montrose, John Wesley
    See Wimberly
Moodey, J. S.—3
Moodey, Kay—1
Moody, Margaret—1
Moor, George—1
Moore, Elvin Edward—1
Moore, Nicholas—5
Moore, Virginia—1
Morden, Phyllis B.—3
Morgan, James—1
Morgan, Jennie—1
Moritz, Genevieve Richards—2
Morley, Frances—2
Morrill, Jane—3
Morrison, Estelle R.—1
Morrison, N. A.
    *R. N. Oliver—1
Morrow, Edward—2
Morrow, Margaret—1
Morse, Irl—1
Morton, David—1
Moser, Alice—2
Mott, Frank Luther—1
Mozer, Anatole—1
Muilenburg, Cornelius Marion—2
Muller, Edwin—1
Mullin, Cora Phebe—1
Mumford, Edwin—1
Murphy, Dennis—1
Murphy, John Maher—1
Murray, Philip—1
Musick, Ruth Ann—1
Nadig, Henry Davis—1
Natanson, Maurice—2
Nathan, Norman—1
Natkins, Miriam—1
Nebraska Writers' Project—1
Neider, Charles—2
Neihardt, John G.—1

Nelson, Pearl M.—1
Newman, Israel—1
Newton, Wesley—1
Norris, Hoke—3
Nutt, Howard—3
O'Brien, Lawrence J.—2
Odell, R. Irvington—1
Ogden, Boyd R.—2
O'Hagen, Howard—1
O'Hara, Joy—1
Oldfield, Barney—1
Olineck, Harriett Scott—1
*Oliver, R. N.
    See Morrison
Olson, James C.—1
Olson, Ted—(1)
Ornstein, William—2
Orr, Cal—1
Orr, Douglass—1
Osborne, Kelsie Ramey—2
Otway, Howard—1
Owens, Grace Mae—1
Palmer, Winthrop—2
Panter, Wayne—2
Paquette, Donald J.—1
Paradise, Jean—1
Park, Dorothy G.—1
Parker, Tim—2
Parrott, Allen—1
Parsons, M. Holmes—3
Patchen, Kenneth—2
Patterson, Charles H.—4
Payne, Maidi—1
Paz, Octavio—1
Peacock, Ray—1
Pearson, Lorene—1
*Pendleton, Conrad
    See Kidd
Pendleton, Paul E.—1
Perkins, Dwight—1
Perlis, Rosella—1
Perry, Merle—2
Peterson, Martin Severin—13
Peterson, William—5
Petri, Lori—5
Pettigrew, Richard C.—1
Petty, Denise—2
Petty, Ford—1
Pfeiler, William K.—2
Phelps, Robert—1
Phillips, Howard W.—1
Pillin, William—1
Pinkney, Dorothy Cowles—1
Piper, Edwin Ford—1 (1)

Piper, Janet—3
Pitzer, Margaret L.—1
Pitzer, R. C.—3
Podair, S[imon]—1
Pogarsky, Solomon—1
Polk, Marguerite—1
Polsky, Thomas—2
Ponedel, Ivan M.—1
Poole, Mary—2
Pope, Clifford H.
    See Adams
Pope, Jack—3
Post, Mary Brinker—2
Pound, Louise—2
Powell, Clarence Alva—2
Powell, Floyd T.—4
Prescott, Russell T.—5
Prochnow, Herbert V.—1
Prosper, Joan Dareth—(1)
Provines, Mary Virginia—1
Pruitt, Robert—1
Pulos, C. E.—3
Purdy, James—1
Purintun, Theodore—1
Quick, Dorothy—2
Quinn, Alberta—1
Quinn, Kerker—1
Raiziss, S[onia]—1
Ramsden, Howard—5
Randall, Kenneth C.—1
Randall, R. L.—1
Rapp, Albert—1
Raymund, Bernard—4
Read, Martha—1
Read, Virginia—1
Reece, Byron Herbert—9
Reese, John Henry—3
Reinhardt, James M.—4
Renwick, Cyra—1
Resneck, Daniel H.—1
Reynard, Peter—(1)
Reynolds, Bryan—2
Rhodes, Barbara—1
Rhodes, Mary K.—2
Richards, Chris—2
*Richards, Mansell—1
Richards, Robert F.—1
Richards, Rosemonde E.—2
Richardson, Chalmer O.—1
Rinaldy, Virginia—1
Rinear, Roberta—1
Ríos, Teré—2
Ritchie, Douglas—1
Riter, Faye—2

Robbins, Polly—1
Roberts, Hortense Roberta—1
Robertson, Gladys Vondy—1
Robson, Merritt—1
Rogers, Julia Anne—1
Rogers, Paul H.—1
Roper, Murray J.—1
Roscoe, Stelle—2
Rosene, Michael—3
Rosewater, Barbara McAlvoy—3
Roskolenko, Harry—3
Ross, Lyman L.—3
Rosse, James C.—4
Rundell, E. Ralph—1
Russ, Elmo—1
Russell, Bayka—1
Russell, Charles B.—1
Russell, Ethel Green—2
Russell, Helen M.—1
Russell, Sydney King—1
Ryan, Thomas G.—1
Ryan, William G.—1
Rydell, Helen Bullard—4
Salinger, Herman—2
Saltzman, Eleanor—6
Sampley, Arthur M.—1
Samuels, Victoria—1
Sandahl, Cliff—1
Sandoz, Mari—3
    See also Macumber
Sarett, Lew—(1)
Scales, Helen—1
Schaupp, Roscoe F.—1
Schaupp, Zora—1
Schellin, Ruth—1
Scherrebeck, Thomas—1
Schmidt, Alex R.—6
Scholten, Libbie Breuer—1
Scholten, Martin—3
Schorer, Mark—1
Schossberger, Emily—4
Schulman, Sam—1
Schwartz, Elias—1
Schweninger, Ivan—3
Scott, Hardiman—1
Scott, R. E.—1
Scott, Winfield Townley—2
Sealock, Nancy W.—1
Sealock, Thelma W.—2
Sears, Paul B.—1
Sellinger, Caryl—1
Sellerier, Bobette—1
Sellerier, Don C.—1
Sellers, J. L.—1

Senior, Edward—2
Shankland, Katherine—1
Shanklin, Jay—1
Shanklin, Maxine—1
Sharp, Craig—1
Shattuck, Katharine—2
Shaw, Dorothy Scott—1
Shaw, Eileen—2
Shaw, Elizabeth—1
Shaw, Fred—2
Shedd, Harrison Graves—1
Sheehy, James A.
    See MacDonald
Sheffield, Robert—1
Shelburne, Mary Willis—3
Shelby, K. C.—1
Sherman, George Witter—2
Sherman, Lucius A.—7
Sherry, Ruth Forbes—4
Shields, Currin—1
Shillington, James K.—1
Shirek, Brownlee—3
Shively, James R.—1
Shokes, C. D.—1
Shriver, Ruth Estelle—3
Sigmund, Jay G.—(1)
Sikes, C. Ernest—2
Silliman, Charles A.—1
Sisk, John P.—5
Skapski, Adam
    *S. Adam—2
Sloane, Charles—1
Slote, Bernice—6
Smith, Catherine Ruth—4
Smith, Dale—1
Smith, David Hubbard
    *Walker Wheatland—1
Smith, James Steel—1
Smith, LeRoy, Jr.—1
Smith, Lewis Worthington—4
Smith, Linus Burr—1
Smith, Maude S.—3
Smith, Sprague O.—1
Snell, George—1
Sohlberg, A. Theodore—1
Solana, Rafael—1
Sonderegger,Leo—8
    *Gulliver—1
Sorenson, Robert—1
Spencer, Josephine—1
Spingarn, Lawrence Perry—3
Squires, Edith Lombard—1
Stacton, David Derek—2
Stafford, William—1

Stait, Virginia—(1)
Stancill, Margaret—2
Standen, Robert Ellis—1
Stanley, Marion Edward—4
Stanley-Clark, A. R.
    —and William B. Thomas—1
Steele, Ralph—1
Stefan, Karl—1
Stepanek, Orin—2
Stephens, Genevieve K.—1
Stephens, George Darwin—1
Stepp, Edward Frank—1
Sterling, Pan M.—3
Stevens, Cj—2
Stevenson, Candace Thurber—2
Stewart, Rex—1
Stewart, Winifred Gray—14
Still, James—2
Stockwell, Esther Price—1
Stoke, Harold W.—1
Stough, Robert Paul—2
Stowe, Ethel Gertrude—1
Streng, John F.—1
Strong, Samuel M.—1
Stuart, Jeb—4
Stuart, Jesse—8
Stuff, Marjorie Ann—1
Sturgis, Robert—1
Suesens, John—2
Sullivan, A. M.—1
Sullivan, E. A.—1
Sullivan, Richard—1
Summers, Hollis—1
Sunwall, James—1
Surmelian, Leon Z.—4
Sutton, Kathleen—3
Swallow, Alan—5
Swan, Charles L.—1
Swenson,A. C. R.—1
Tallant, Robert—1
Talmadge, John E.—1
Talt, Philip—1
Tashner, Martin—1
Tate, Leonard L.—1
Taylor, K. P. A.—1
Taylor, Mykia—1
Tekeyan, Charles—1
Tempest, Michael—3
Templin, E. H.—2
Terrell, Upton—1
Thayer, Harriet—1
Thomas, Dorothy—3
Thomas, Jean—1
Thomas, Kenetha—1

Thomas, Macklin—4
Thomas, William Burl—1
Thompson, Adele Kelley—1
Thompson, C. Hall—1
Thompson, Jim—4
Thompson, Mary Agnes—2
Thompson, Robert E.—1
Thompson, William F.—1
Thompson, Rosamund Dargan—3
Thomson, S. Harrison—1
Thorpe, Iris Lora—2
Thurin, Ena—1
Thurston, Nita Muriel—1
Tilghman, Zoe A.—1
Tinsley, Herbert—2
Todd, Helen—1
Torrey, Volta—1
Totman, James M.—1
Towley, Louis—1
Triem, Eve—1
Trowbridge, W. D.—1
Truslow, Marguerite W.—1
Turner, Raymond O.—1
Tuttle, Stella Weston—1
Tvrdik, Harriet Adams—1
Uhlarik, Carl—4
Uhler, John Earle—1
Umland, Rudolph—24
Underwood, Charlene—1
Underwood, John E.—1
Uschold, Maud E.—4
Uzzell, Thomas H.—1
Valyear, Howard—1
Van Atta, Winfred L.—2
Van Deusen, Delia—1
Van Dine, Warren L.—1
*Vane, Arthur—1
Van Liew, James—1
VanMale, John—3
Van Wyck, Eleanor—1
Viereck, Peter—4
Villa, José Garcia
   See Garcia Villa
Vinal, Harold—18 (2)
Voorhees, Richard J.—1
*W., H.—2
Waggoner, Frances—1
Waldron, Eli—2
Waldron, Webb
   See Calkins
Walker, Faye Chilcote—3
Wall, Ben M.—1
Wallace, Alfonz—4
Wallach, Ira Jan—1

Waller, Willard—1
Wallis, Eleanor Glenn—2
Walt, Bobby—1
Walton, Mary Ethel—1
Ward, Leo R.—2
Ward, William Allen—1
Ware, Althea—1
Warren, James E., Jr.—1
Wassall, Irma—2
*Wassenaar, Ruurd—1
Waters, Bruce—2
Watson, Editha L.—1
Way, Leah—1
Weathers, Winston—7
*Weaver, Anna—1
Weaver, Bennet—(1)
Weber, Lee Andrew—1
Webster, Wilfrid—2
Webster, Winifred F.—1
Wedel, Waldo R.—1
Weil, Leonard Dankmar—1
Weismiller, Edward—1
Weiss, Henry George—2
Welch, Marie DeL.—1 (2)
Wellington, Grace Kemmerling—1
Welty, Eudora—3
Wentz, Paul P.—1
*Wert, Sarah E.—1
West, Harry L.—2
West, Jessamyn—1
West, Ray B., Jr.—4
West, V. Royce—1
Westbrook, John T.—5
Wetjen, Albert Richard—(1)
*Wheatland, Walker
   See Smith, David
Whelan, Kenneth—1
White, May Smith—1
Whitehand, Robert—2
Whiteley, Mary N. S.—1
Whitton, Mary Ormsbee—1
Widdemer, Margaret—(1)
Wiggam, Lionel—1
Wilder, Leland—1
Wildey, Iva Lou—1
Wildman, John Hazard—2
Wilhelmson, Virginia—1
Wilkins, E. Michael—1
Williams, Ann—1
Williams, Clinton—4
Williams, Harry—1
Williams, Oscar—2
Williams, Patricia—1
Williams, Tennessee—1

Wilson, Harold S.—1
Wilson, John W.—1
Wilson, W. W.—1
Wimberly, Hal B.—1
Wimberly, Lowry C.—17
    *John Wesley Montrose—1
    *Lathrop Q. Merriwell—2
    *Van Martin Dexter—1
Wimberly, May Boynton—1
Wing, Maurice J.—1
Winslow, Kathryn—3
Winslow, Walker—4
Winters, Elizabeth R.—2
Witt, Harold V.—3
Wittmann, Elizabeth—1
Wolf, Michael—1
Wood, Allyn—1
Woodmency, Don—1
Woolf, Douglas G., Jr.—1

Wright, Alice—1
Wright, Bennett—1
Wright, Celeste Turner—1
Wright, Jacqueline—2
Wright, Walter F.—4
Wright, William—1
Wyckoff, Jane Morrill
    See Morrill
Yates, Elizabeth Crawford—3
Yates, Paulene M.—1
Yauger, Fay M.—1
Yeatman, Jeannette—1
Yenne, Herbert—1
Yuan, Chen-Shih—2
Zacks, Robert—2
Zahn, Curtis—1
Zalburg, Sanford—1
Zukerman, William—3

C

MEMBERS OF THE STAFF

All people who served on the staff of the *Prairie Schooner* during its
first twenty-five years are listed below according to the capacity in which
they served. Under each division they are listed in the chronological
order of their joining the staff. Duration of service is indicated by inclusive issues. To avoid confusion, temporary variations in title have been
ignored, and all staff members have been listed under the title normally
assigned to their positions.

Editor

    Lowry C. Wimberly (January, 1927—   )

Associate Editors

    Roscoe F. Schaupp (January, 1927—July, 1927)
    Jacob H[arris] Gable (January, 1927—February, 1928)
    Marion Edward Stanley (January, 1927)
    Volta Torrey (Januuary, 1927)
    Martin Severin Peterson (April, 1927—Winter, 1941)
    Gayle C. Walker (April, 1927)
    Robert N. Lasch (July, 1927—Spring, 1928)
    Wilfred Webster (July, 1927—Spring, 1928)
    Loren C. Eiseley (October, 1927; Fall, 1928—Winter, 1929)
    Gilbert H. Doane (October, 1927—Fall, 1928)
    Wilbur G. Gaffney (October, 1927—Spring, 1928)
    Ivan Hall (October, 1927—Winter, 1928)
    Russell T[rue] Prescott (Summer, 1928—Winter, 1941)
    Adrian Ehrenberger (Fall, 1928)
    Clifford Sandahl (Fall, 1928)
    Frederick L. Christensen (Fall, 1928—   )
    Don Carlos Sellerier (Fall, 1928—Fall, 1929)
    Gerald V. Humbert (Winter, 1930)
    Paul Gillan (Spring, 1930—Fall, 1931)
    Willard F. Gostelow (Summer, 1930—Fall, 1931)
    Norman E. Eliason (Fall, 1930—Summer, 1932)
    John Suesens (Winter, 1932—Summer, 1933)
    Lowell Thomas (Winter, 1932—Spring, 1932)
    Margaret Deming (Summer, 1932—Summer, 1933; Summer, 1934—
      Winter, 1935)
    Dorothy Cook (Summer, 1932—Spring, 1934)
    Gwendolyn B. Thompson (Fall, 1933—Spring, 1934)

Maurice O. Johnson (Fall, 1933–Spring, 1938)
Pearl Joan Cosgrave (Fall, 1933–Fall, 1937)
Paul Barrons (Fall, 1933–Spring, 1934)
Margaret Cannell (Summer, 1934–Winter, 1936)
Louise Perry (Winter, 1935–Winter, 1940)
Grace Owens (Winter, 1935–Fall, 1940)
Edith Grobmann (Spring, 1937–Fall, 1937)
V. Royce West (Fall, 1938–Winter, 1940)
Leo Sonderegger (Spring, 1940–Summer, 1941)
Eleanor H. Ambuhl (Winter, 1940–Summer, 1941)
Arthur F. Jenness (Winter, 1942–Winter, 1946)
James Lee Sellers (Winter, 1942–Winter, 1946)
Gretchen Burnham (Winter, 1945–Winter, 1948)

Contributing Editors

Gilbert H. Doane (Winter, 1929–Summer, 1937)
Loren C. Eiseley (Winter, 1929–Winter, 1939)
Weldon Kees (Winter, 1937–Winter, 1939)

Advisory Editors (also called "Honorary Editors")

Lucius Adelno Sherman (January, 1927–Winter, 1933)
Robert Douglas Scott (January, 1927–Winter, 1940)
John G. Neihardt (April, 1927–   )
Gayle C. Walker (October, 1927–Fall, 1941)
V. Royce West (October, 1927–Fall, 1928)
Roscoe Schaupp (October, 1927–Summer, 1930)
Robert P. Crawford (Summer, 1928–Winter, 1940; Summer, 1942–
    Winter, 1946; Fall, 1948–   )
J. E. LeRossignol (Winter, 1929–Winter, 1946)
J[acob] Harris Gable (Winter, 1929–Spring, 1933)
Thomas M. Raysor (Fall, 1930–   )
Ray W. Frantz (Spring, 1941–   )
Carroll Chouinard (Spring, 1941–Fall, 1941)
Emily Schossberger (Winter, 1941–   )
Boyd Carter (Fall, 1948–   )

Business Managers

V. Royce West (January, 1927–July, 1927)
Roland Miller (October, 1927–Spring, 1928)
Philip David Blake (October, 1927–Winter, 1929)
Joe Deming (Spring, 1928–Winter, 1929)
Ted Hartman (Spring, 1929–Summer, 1929)
C. Ernest Sikes (Fall, 1929–Spring, 1930)

Alan G. Williams (Summer, 1930—Winter, 1932)
George Dunn (Fall, 1930—Winter, 1931)
V. M. Butt (Winter, 1930)
Harry H. Foster (Spring, 1932—Summer, 1934)
Harry A. Soderlund (Spring, 1932—Summer, 1932)
Stuart Neitzel (Fall, 1932—Winter, 1934)
Herbert P. Behlen (Summer, 1934—Fall, 1935)
Franklin Smith (Spring, 1936—Fall, 1936)
Lyle C. Fitch (Winter, 1936—Summer, 1937)
Florence Mosher (Winter, 1936—Summer, 1937)
Norman Bolker (Fall, 1937)
Robert Seidel (Winter, 1937—Winter, 1938)
Jack Naber (Spring, 1939)
Keith Brown (Winter, 1939—Fall, 1941)
Ann Keith (Winter, 1939—Summer, 1940)
Charles B. Russell (Winter, 1940)
Frank Bstandig (Winter, 1941—Summer, 1942)
Kurt Porjes (Winter, 1942)
Joanna Radke (Spring, 1943—Summer, 1944)
Margaret Seely (Fall, 1943—Spring, 1944)
Margaret Turner (Summer, 1944—Winter, 1947)
Helen Sill (Spring, 1948)
Gertrude A. Dixon (Summer, 1948—Fall, 1948)
Sicily Ewing (Winter, 1948)
Dorothy C. Barnett (Spring, 1949—Summer, 1949)
Geraldine Soutas Shaffer Ganjei (Fall, 1949—Winter, 1949)
Mrs. John Connelly (Spring, 1950)
Anne Harder (Summer, 1950)
Earle B. Wilson (Fall, 1950—Summer, 1952)

BIBLIOGRAPHY

BIBLIOGRAPHY

The information contained in this study has, for the most part, been derived from an examination of primary sources: the first twenty-five volumes of the *Prairie Schooner*, complete or partial files of some sixty other magazines, newspaper files, and over 2,000 letters in the possession of Dr. Lowry C. Wimberly. As noted above, much information not the subject of written records has been obtained through interviews with Dr. Wimberly. In addition, the following listed secondary sources have contributed, directly or indirectly, to this study.

BOOKS

America Is West, edited with introduction by John T. Flanagan, Minneapolis: University of Minnesota Press, 1945.

American Local-Color Stories, edited with introduction by Harry R. Warfel and G. Harrison Orians, New York: American Book Co., 1941.

American Writing . . . The Anthology and Yearbook of the American Non-commercial Magazine, edited by Alan Swallow, Boston: Bruce Humphries, 1942-1944.

Anderson, Margaret, *My Thirty Years' War,* New York: Covici, Friede, 1930.

Anthology of Magazine Verse . . . and Yearbook of American Poetry, edited by Alan Frederick Pater, New York: The Poetry Digest Association, 1936, 1937; The Paebar Co., 1938, 1942.

Baker, Denys Val, *Little Reviews: 1914-1943,* London: George Allen & Unwin Ltd., 1943.

Best American Short Stories . . . and the Yearbook of the American Short Story, edited by Edward J. O'Brien (1915-1941) and Martha Foley (1942-1952), New York: Dodd, Mead & Co., 1915-1932; Boston: Houghton Mifflin Co., 1933-1952.

Best Poems of . . . , edited by Thomas Moult, New York: Harcourt, Brace & Co., 1926-1942.

Clark, Emily, *Innocence Abroad,* New York and London: Alfred A. Knopf, 1931.

Cooke, George Willis, *An Historical and Biographical Introduction to Accompany the Dial as Reprinted in Numbers for the Rowfant Club* (2 vols.), Cleveland: The Rowfant Club, 1902.

Cowley, Malcolm, *Exile's Return* (Revised Edition), New York: Viking Press, 1951.

Drewry, John E., *Contemporary American Magazines: A Selected Bibliography and Reprints of Articles Dealing with Various Periodicals*, Athens: University of Georgia Press, 1938.

————, *Some Magazines and Magazine Makers*, Boston: The Stratford Co., 1924.

Fletcher, John Gould, *Life Is My Song*, New York and Toronto: Farrar & Rinehart, 1937.

Ford, Ford Madox, *Return to Yesterday*, New York: H. Liveright, Inc., 1932.

Fox, Marjorie Eileen, *William Marion Reedy and the St. Louis Mirror* (M. A. thesis), University of Illinois, 1947.

Freeman, Joseph, *An American Testament: A Narrative of Rebels and Romantics*, New York: Farrar & Rinehart, 1936.

The Fugitive: Clippings and Comment, edited by Merrill Moore, with post-script by John Crowe Ransom, Boston (private), 1939.

Garland, Hamlin, *Crumbling Idols*, with introduction by Robert E. Spiller, Gainesville: Scholars Facsimiles & Reprints, 1952.

Granger's Index to Poetry, edited by Raymond J. Dixon, New York: Columbia University Press, 1953.

Hoffman, Frederick J., Charles Allen, and Carolyn F. Ulrich, *The Little Magazine: A History and a Bibliography*, Princeton: Princeton University Press, 1947.

Kazin, Alfred, *On Native Grounds: An Interpretation of Modern American Prose Literature*, New York: Reynal & Hitchcock, 1942.

Literary Prizes and Their Winners, edited by Anne J. Richter, New York: R. R. Bowker Co., 1946.

The Little Review Anthology, edited with preface and commentary by Margaret Anderson, New York: Hermitage House, 1953.

Mid Country, edited by Lowry C. Wimberly, with introduction by B. A. Botkin, Lincoln: University of Nebraska Press, 1945.

Minor, Benjamin Blake, *The Southern Literary Messenger: 1834-1864*, New York and Washington: Neale Publishing Co., 1905.

Monroe, Harriet, *A Poet's Life: Seventy Years in a Changing World*, New York: The Macmillan Co., 1938.

Moore, Harry E., *What Is Regionalism?*, Chapel Hill: University of North Carolina Press, 1937.

Nebraska Blue Book, Lincoln: Nebraska Legislative Reference Bureau, 1926, 1928.

O. Henry Memorial Award Anthology . . . , edited by Blanche Colton Williams (1919-1932) *et al.*, New York: Doubleday, Doran & Co., 1919-1952.

Out of the Midwest, edited with introduction by John T. Frederick, New York and London: Whittlesey House, 1944.

The Partisan Reader, edited by William Phillips and Philip Rahv, with introduction by Lionel Trilling, New York: Dial Press, 1946.

Poetry Awards . . . , edited by Robert Moore, Philadelphia: University of Pennsylvania Press, 1949, 1950.

Prairie Schooner Caravan, edited by Lowry C. Wimberly, with introduction by Dorothy Canfield Fisher, Lincoln: University of Nebraska Press, 1943.

Regionalism in America, edited by Merrill Jensen, with foreword by Felix Frankfurter, Madison: University of Wisconsin Press, 1951.

Rocky Mountain Reader, edited with introduction by Ray B. West, Jr., New York: E. P. Dutton & Co., 1946.

Short Story Hits . . . An Interpretative Anthology, edited by Thomas H. Uzzell, New York: Harcourt Brace & Co., 1933, 1934.

Short Story Index, compiled by Dorothy E. Cook and Isabel S. Monro, New York: H. W. Wilson Co., 1953.

Tietjens, Eunice, *The World at My Shoulder,* New York: The Macmillan Co., 1938.

Turner, Alice Lucile, *A Study of the Content of the Sewanee Review with Historical Introduction,* Nashville: George Peabody College for Teachers, 1931.

Untermeyer, Louis, *From Another World,* New York: Harcourt, Brace & Co., 1939.

Williams, William Carlos, *The Autobiography of William Carlos Williams,* New York: Random House, 1952.

ARTICLES

Allen, Charles, "Regionalism and the Little Magazines," *College English,* VII, 10-16 (October, 1945).

Allen, Frederick L., "The American Magazine Grows Up," *Atlantic Monthly,* CLXXX, 76-82 (November, 1947).

Arrowsmith, William, *"Partisan Review* and American Writing," *Hudson Review,* I, 526-537 (Winter, 1948).

Baker, Carlos, "Delineation of Life and Character," *Literary History of the United States,* edited by Robert E. Spiller *et al.,* New York: The Macmillan Co., 1948, II, 843-861.

Bixler, Paul, "Little Magazine, What Now?" *Antioch Review,* VIII, 63-77 (Spring, 1948).

Clough, W. O., "Regionalism," *Rocky Mountain Review,* III, 1-2 (Winter, 1938-39).

Cowley, Malcolm, "The Little Magazines Growing Up," New York *Times Book Review,* September 14, 1947, p. 35.

————, "Magazine Business: 1910-46," *New Republic,* CXV, 521-523 (October 21, 1946) .

Dillon, George, "The 'Little Magazine' Gimmick," *Poetry,* LXXI, 41-44 (October, 1947).

Eliot, T. S., "The Idea of a Literary Review," *Criterion,* IV, 1-6 (January, 1926) .

Flanagan, John T., "Early Literary Periodicals in Minnesota," *Minnesota History,* XXVI, 293-311 (December, 1945) .

"The Great Midwest Book Shelf," Chicago *Sun Book Week,* May 4, 1947. (This 24-page special issue of the *Book Week* contains articles by twenty-six authors, all dealing with some aspect of Midwestern literature.)

Hartley, Lois T., "The *Midland,*" *Iowa Journal of History,* XLVII, 325-344 (October, 1949).

Hemens, R. D., "Magazines That Come Off the Presses," *Saturday Review of Literature,* XXIX, 11 (June 8, 1946).

Heine, Emily, "Ripe Old Age of 25," Omaha *World-Herald Magazine,* June 24, 1951, p. 5.

Johnson, Maurice O., "The *Prairie Schooner:* Ten Years," *Prairie Schooner,* XI, 71-82 (Spring, 1937).

Kees, Weldon, "Magazine Chronicle," *Prairie Schooner,* XIII, 66-68 (Spring, 1939) .

Knickerbocker, W. S., "Up from the South," *Western Review,* XIII, 168-178 (Spring, 1949).

Lyon, Mary, "The College Magazine—and After," *Mademoiselle,* XXIX, 250-251, 340-346 (August, 1949).

Matthiessen, F. O., "Poetry," *Literary History of the United States,* edited by Robert E. Spiller *et al.,* New York: The Macmillan Co., 1948, II, 1335-1357.

Mims, Edwin, "Early Years of the *South Atlantic Quarterly,*" *South Atlantic Quarterly,* LI, 33-63 (January, 1952) .

O'Connor, William Van, "Little Magazines in the Third Generation," *Poetry,* LXXIII, 367-369 (March, 1949) .

————, "Recent Magazines: The Expense of Conventions," *Poetry,* LXXVI, 118-120 (May, 1950).

Peterson, Martin S., "Regional Magazines," *Prairie Schooner,* III, 292-295 (Fall, 1929).

Ransom, John Crowe, *et al.,* "The Misery and Necessity of the Quarterly," *American Scholar,* XV, 550-554 (Autumn, 1946).

Sandoz, Mari, *"Folk-Say,"* *Prairie Schooner,* VI, 65-67 (Winter, 1932).

Smith, Henry Nash, "The Frontier Hypothesis and the Myth of the West," *American Quarterly*, II, 3-11 (Spring, 1950).

Stegner, Wallace, "Western Record and Romance," *Literary History of the United States*, edited by Robert E. Spiller *et al.*, New York: The Macmillan Co., 1948, II, 862-877.

Swallow, Alan, "The Little Magazines," *Prairie Schooner*, XVI, 238-243 (Winter, 1942).

————, "Postwar Little Magazines," *Prairie Schooner*, XXIII, 152-157 (Summer, 1949).

Tate, Allen, "The New Provincialism," *Virginia Quarterly Review*, XXI, 262-272 (Spring, 1945).

Towne, C. H., "The One-Man Magazines," *American Mercury*, LXIII, 104-108 (July, 1946).

Vivas, Eliseo, "Criticism and the Little Magazines," *Western Review*, XVI, 2-11 (Autumn, 1951).

Wimberly, Lowry Charles, "Midland Regionalism," Chicago *Sun Book Week*, December 2, 1945, p. 4.

Winther, Sophus K., "The Limits of Regionalism," *Arizona Quarterly*, VIII, 30-36 (Spring, 1952).

Wright, Louella M., "The *Midland Monthly*," *Iowa Journal of History and Politics*, XLV, 3-61 (January, 1947).

Zabel, Morton D., "Summary in Criticism," *Literary History of the United States*, edited by Robert E. Spiller *et al.*, New York: The Macmillan Co., 1948, II, 1358-1373.